RESEARCH GUIDE IN
speech

RESEARCH GUIDE IN
speech

184901

Gerilyn Tandberg
Louisiana State University, Baton Rouge

Consulting Editor: Carl Kalvelage

GENERAL LEARNING PRESS
250 James Street
Morristown, New Jersey 07960

Preface

People of all ages and in all walks of life need to know how to speak in public. A student may be called upon to deliver an oral report. A housewife may find it necessary to run a public meeting. A politician, by definition, must be an able public speaker. This research guide is an attempt to provide a rapid overview of basic concepts as well as a comprehensive list of references that can help both the beginning and advanced speaker.

This book includes all the information that a beginning student will need in order to find and develop a topic, to prepare and deliver speeches. A chart provides a bird's-eye view of the major ideas and techniques, while short sections cover discussion, debate, radio and television speaking, oral interpretation of literature, group reading, and reader's theater.

There are also special features, more specific in nature, that would be of particular interest to students majoring or minoring in the field of speech. Footnote and bibliography forms are given as well as a listing of annotated reference works in both general and specific fields where acceptable speeches may be found. Also included are an annotated bibliography of reference works, journals, and new textbooks in the area of speech communication, tips for successful interviewing and for correspondence with government officials, and a list of addresses to national and international interest groups. In a detailed chart are delineated great orators and theoreticians, their dates, works, characteristics, and motivations and/or philosophies, and another chart deals with the different approaches to rhetorical criticism.

Active young people today are reluctant to spend hours reading a textbook. They want the information to be concise and to the point, easily applicable to their immediate problem of preparing a speech, a discussion, or a debate. This research guide will help them accomplish their goal.

Acknowledgements

Certain material included in this book is copyrighted by the authors and publishers of the following citations. The use of these editions is gratefully acknowledged.

Kalvelage, Carl, Segal, Morley, and Anderson, Peter J. *Research Guide for Undergraduates in Political Science.* Morristown, N.J.: General Learning Press, 1972.

Oliver, Robert T. "The Eternal (and Infernal) Problem of Grades," *The Speech Teacher,* IX (January, 1960):9-10.

Scott, Robert L. and Brock, Bernard L. *Methods of Rhetorical Criticism: A Twentieth Century Perspective.* New York: Harper & Row, 1972.

A number of colleagues and friends have given valuable suggestions and assistance in the preparation of the book. Professor Ernest Bormann's (University of Minnesota) comments were especially helpful. Junnell Podominick's were similarly comprehensive and valuable. Others to be acknowledged for their contributions are Steve Mattern and the consulting editor, Carl Kalvelage. Special acknowledgement for her research assistance and editing is given to Carol Rothkopf.

Finally, I would recognize the fact that she to whom this book is dedicated, along with my mother and father, imparted to me the basic attitudes, ideals and motivations that made possible my undertaking the project. I alone remain responsible for all errors of fact and judgement.

Dedicated to my grandmother, Christina Lunde

Contents

Part I

HOW TO RESEARCH, WRITE, & DELIVER A SPEECH

The Concept and History of Communication

AN INTRODUCTION TO THE CONCEPT OF COMMUNICATION

Communication has so many dimensions that it can be given no simple definition. Basically it is an expression of oneself. It might be a symphony, a painting, a theatrical production, a look, or a gesture. But it is only through the process of speaking in a social setting that there can be the intimate and spontaneous interaction that keeps people from feeling isolated. Communication in this social context is the focus of this book.

Symbols

The process begins with an idea conceived in the mind of an individual. It can only be transmitted to another person after it has been converted into a physical form through symbols. These symbols are words organized in a pattern that communicate the idea. The symbols give structure to the idea, helping the audience to understand what is being said.

Point of View and Strategy

Another important element in the communication process is point of view. This can be described as the particular stance, or attitude that has been adopted by the speaker or the person spoken to as a result of any number of factors such as environmental conditions, group controls, or individual differences. If these factors interfere with communication and acceptance of the message, they and any other disruption, such as unclear speech construction, may create friction. These factors are the best reason for using strategy in word choice and overall organization. If strategy is not used, the speaker may not be able to persuade the listener that his ideas are worth hearing.

Semantics

The listener may misconstrue the speaker's meaning if strategy is not used. Many times, however, even the best strategy will be ineffective because the words clash. Concrete words communicate best. They have a clear-cut dictionary definition. After all, everyone is familiar with basic concept of a chair. On the other hand, abstract words such as love, duty, honor, and democracy cannot be defined so closely. Everyone has his own concept of these terms. Connotations confuse the issue even more. Usage has added emotional meanings to words—meanings that usually have nothing to do with the dictionary definition. Therefore a word like "chicken," which has a dictionary meaning (a two-legged barnyard fowl, etc.), can also connote cowardice. If all connotatively favorable or unfavorable terms could be distinguished this easily, communication problems would not be so great. But each human being, because of his background, will have his own reaction to particular words. To one person the word "sophisticated" might conjure up an image of a stuffy-looking man with an immaculate suit, eyeglasses, and tightly furled umbrella; to somebody else it may be a beautifully gowned and coiffed woman who is in command of any situation.

Feedback

In any case, the transmitter who is sending the message will receive feedback, or a counter message, from the receiver that may consist merely of a look or a gesture. If the transmitter is alive and aware, he will be able to gauge this response and alter the wording, organization, or tone of his message accordingly. Because of this complicated procedure, transmission can be called a bi-directional process. Signals are passed both from and to the transmitter.

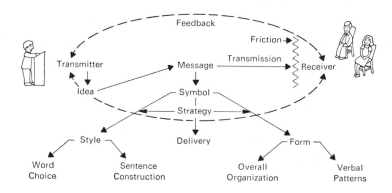

HISTORY OF RHETORIC

People of all ages and nationalities have employed this communication process. Rhetoricians of the past had different motivations and used various strategies and oratorical skills to get their points across. Many people today believe that our society can learn to improve on its communication techniques by reexamining those of the past. The orators of ancient Greece and Rome refined communication skills to the point where they became an art. Since many of the topics were both vital and timely, a history of all the orators and their speech topics amounts to a political, social, and economic history of their nations and of the world.

A list of many (not all) of the world's leading speakers and theoreticians is in Part IV, starting on p. 181, of this research guide. The chart is divided into different historical periods. The nationality of each speaker along with his major works and outstanding communication characteristics, their significance, and some of the motivations for his speaking will be found grouped according to historical period.

Selecting, Developing, and Researching a Topic

UNDERSTANDING POINTS OF STRATEGY AND SELECTING A TOPIC

Although strategies and techniques have differed through the ages, several underlying concepts are common to the communication process in all periods. There must be an idea and a plan to convey that idea as effectively as possible to the listener.

The topic is one aspect of the idea. Its form, as can be seen in table 1, is a phrase, and it is focused and communicated through its thesis (see p. 8) and organization. The three major strategic considerations are the speaker, the occasion, and the audience. These determine the topic, purpose, thesis, organization, techniques, style (word choice and sentence structure), and delivery.

The Speaker Determines the Topic

The speaker must first ask himself if he is interested in his topic and if he believes in his major premise or idea. It is difficult to communicate sincerity or enthusiasm if one does not feel it. The speaker must be objective enough about himself to determine if he has the educational background and intelligence to address himself to his topic. He must analyze the audience to determine if he will be acceptable to it. Audiences will usually listen attentively to someone they know and respect.

Know Your Audience

If a speaker wishes to be successful, he also must analyze the audience's characteristics. It must be approached as a unit. For example, if a speaker chooses the American theater as his topic, he must consider whether his audience is composed of rural or city people; laymen or professionals. It would be unwise to talk in depth about off-Broadway productions to a midwestern audience unfamiliar with such plays. Technical terms and phrases must be avoided with non-specialist audiences; similarly, complex ideas should be avoided or simplified with unsophisticated audiences. Individual attitudes and interests must be remembered, too. These major factors for consideration of the audience are listed in the far right column of table 1.

Matching the Topic and the Occasion

Occasion is a concept alluding to all of the circumstances that bring a speech into existence. Major factors that compose an occasion are the temper of the times, the setting, group size, purpose of the meeting, and program agenda.

Every age has its own "temper," which the speaker should take into account when choosing a topic and organizing a speech. "Temper of the times" is a term denoting certain attitudes or emotions that are common to large groups of people at any one time in history. Anti-communist feelings during the McCarthy era in the 1950s in the United States or hostility towards witches in seventeenth-century Salem influenced the way a subject might or might not be treated in those periods. In those eras anyone who vigorously advocated communism or witchcraft would immediately have been suspect and treated in an unfriendly manner. To persuade people to change their views always requires tact.

A setting includes both all-encompassing worldwide, national, and even local events and feelings, and the more specific environment in which the speech is delivered. Occurrences such as storms, holidays, economic or political disruptions are examples of elements in the macroscopic setting that

TABLE 1 / General Speech Summary Table

	General Purpose	General Form	Delivery	Strategy		
				Speaker	Occasion	Audience

TOPIC or SUBJECT		A phrase	Introduced in the thesis and delivered through the organization	Relevance to:
				1. Personal interest
				2. Personal qualifications
				  a. Status
				  b. Education
				  c. Intelligence
				3. Personality
				4. Reputation
				5. Need to express and communicate vs. the need to be safe
					Relevance to:
					1. Purpose of the meeting
					2. Macroscopic setting
					3. Microscopic setting
					4. Group size
					5. Program agenda
					6. The temper of the times
						Relevance to:
						1. Intelligence
						2. Sophistication
						3. General group attitudes and interests
						4. Individual attitudes and interests
						5. Age
						6. Sex
						7. Socioeconomic background

SPECIFIC PURPOSE AND	Inform Entertain Persuade Activate	A phrase	Transmitted, developed and supported through the organization and techniques			
THESIS		A simple, declarative sentence				

ORGANIZA-TION		*Introduction*
		1. Attention Step
		2. Need Step
		3. Statement of Purpose or Thesis
		4. Statement of Outline (optional)
		
		Body
		Types of organization are listed on pages 000-000.
			Especially Important
			1. Vocal Aspect
			  a. Appropriate Volume
			  b. Clear Articulation
			  c. Clear Enunciation
			  d. Proper Pronunciation
			  e. Vocal Variations
			    (1) Timing:
			      Rate
			      Pause			

TABLE 1 / continued

| | General Purpose | General Form | Delivery | Strategy | | |
				Speaker	Occasion	Audience
		Conclusion 1. Summary 2. Recapitulation 3. Application Type 4. Challenge or Appeal 5. Motivation Type 6. Statement of Personal Intentions	Rhythm (2) Pitch (3) Volume (4) Quality 2. Physical Aspects a. Facial Expression b. Eye Contact c. Posture d. Move with motivation			
TECHNIQUES		Types of techniques are listed on pages 000-000.				
STYLE		1. Word Choice 2. Use of Imagery 3. Types of Syntax 4. Variations in Sentences				

may influence audiences. Immediately after the bombing of Pearl Harbor or the assassination of President Kennedy, for instance, it is doubtful if most people in the United States would have wanted to hear a humorous speech.

In order to utilize either the setting for his own purposes or to counteract its liabilities, a speaker must be both alert and versatile. The room may have poor accoustics, be too large for the audience, too shabby for the purpose, too noisy, or too ornate, and thus distract the audience's attention away from the speaker. The group may be a large one calling for a formal presentation, or a small one dictating informality. Furthermore, most meetings are motivated by a particular purpose that should not be overlooked. If, for example, the purpose of the gathering is to negotiate with a striking stagehand crew, the speaker should not be talking about the characteristics of the stage hero of the 1950s. Even the program itself may be distracting. The audience may be looking forward to the next speaker, to dinner, to a floorshow, or merely to getting home. A speaker should consider the program as a whole and speak only during the allotted time. An audience usually appreciates brevity. All of these factors—speaker, audience, and occasion— are found in the upper right corner of table 1. They are major factors to consider when planning the strategy of the entire speech.

The Topic in a Classroom Situation

In the event that a classroom speech is called for, the instructor may assign the topic. Usually, however, the selection of the topic will be left up to the student and it can be a time consuming and frustrating task.

The problem is one of developing a focus that is both interesting to the student speaker and to his audience of classmates; appropriate to his qualifications, the occasion, and the audience; and workable within the time allotted. Hours may be spent trying to formulate an approach or researching what turns out to be an unworkable topic. An interesting topic such as "How to Prevent World War III" may not be manageable. A manageable topic such as "Bolivia and American Tin Quotas" might not stir the imagination. Timely or unusual topics tend to interest audiences the most. In order to discover which topic is timely or unusual to a particular audience, a speaker must analyze the group and occasion according to the categories previously discussed and also listed under the "Audience" and "Occasion" headings on the chart on p. 8. These audience dimensions apply to a classroom audience as much as they do to a regular audience which, for one reason or another, has chosen to come and listen to the speech.

For the speaker's sake, it is important to select a topic that is interesting, not only as it is originally conceived, but that will continue to hold one's interest throughout the hard task of research, organization, and presentation. Choosing a topic and scanning the sources are not separate tasks; they are entwined— doing one helps in doing the other. In the following section three important steps are presented that lead to developing an interesting and workable topic.

A PRACTICAL FORMULA FOR CHOOSING A TOPIC

The first step in developing any formula is to define its elements; thus, one must first decide upon an area to investigate. To simplify this process, possible research areas have been divided into two basic groups: the concrete and the abstract. These two general areas are further divided into subgroups.

The Concrete

There is a natural appeal to a concrete topic that deals with a *person*, an *entity* or *organization*, an *event*, an *object*, or a *law*. If one has a predisposition to investigate something, it is likely to be one of the above concrete items. If the idea of such a topic is appealing, but it is difficult to choose which person or country would be most interesting, an hour or so of creative browsing may be rewarding. Simply thumbing through several of the resources listed in Part II may bring several topics to mind.

The Abstract

Classifying ideas and abstractions has been the pursuit of philosophers for centuries. Since the purpose of this book is to use ideas in a practical fashion to help focus and organize the proposed speech, a very simple three-fold classification will be adopted for abstract topics.

VALUE

This refers to any concept or idea that describes an interest, pleasure, moral obligation, desire, want, need, etc. It may refer to a measurable activity, such as equal opportunity in employment, or to an intangible, such as "support for the regime."

PROBLEM

A problem may also be classified as measurable activity or a feeling; but it is generally regarded as an undesirable, such as a feeling of political alienation, or apathy.

PROCESS

This word has no connotation of desirability or undesirability. It simply refers to any observable or definable pattern in activities of people and groups. "Political process" for example, refers to the pattern that emerges from the behavior of people and groups as they strive for and use political power. Many ideas or concepts can be placed in two or even all three of these categories. How many categories are involved depends upon the speaker's general purpose. The speaker's general purpose is normally fourfold—to inform, to persuade, to motivate to action, and to entertain. The musical philosophy of the Beatles for instance, can be treated as a neutral process; as an affront to the musical world; a boon to contemporary music; or as a phenomena that should not be taken seriously. How one regards these ideas depends upon one's own attitudes. The categories of value, problem, and process simply help in identifying one's own feelings toward these ideas in order to use them in organizing a speech.

DEVELOPING THE TOPIC

As one begins to explore the available material, however, it is usually discovered that far more has been written on the chosen topic than expected. The traditional advice is to "narrow" the topic. What is usually called "narrowing down" refers to the process of reducing a topic in terms of either time, space, or purpose. Narrowing down means limiting the topic or focusing upon a small part of it. Applying a purpose or approach to a topic will help limit it. In other words, a definition is created. In terms of a definition, one chooses the appropriate strategy, which is influenced by the other variables—the audience, occasion, and speaker. Exactly how narrow the topic must be is usually determined by the nature of the occasion and the amount of time allotted to the speech. Instead of speaking about Robert Kennedy's entire life, the topic may be reduced to the months he spent working for Senator Joseph McCarthy. Instead of speaking about Mexican politics, a speech on politics in Sonora province might be developed. The project now appears to become manageable, but it actually may not be, because one still may find that there is far more written about politics in Sonora province or about this period in Robert Kennedy's life than can be dealt with in a fifteen-minute speech. When a topic is finally narrowed down, it often is so narrow that it becomes a task even to state the title. On the other hand, if it is decided not to narrow the topic, coverage is often so superficial that it becomes only a review of available materials and all originality is sacrificed. Another way to reduce a topic to manageable proportions is to develop a sharper focus. Ask yourself interesting and worthwhile questions that might be answered about the chosen topic. These questions should help to define what is relevant and what is not relevant for research. These questions may also lead to a comprehensive thesis.

The problem is now to identify these questions. One method is to combine the categories of the abstract and concrete; for example, that topic of Robert Kennedy (concrete) and the idea of "Black Power" (an abstract value). There are a great many possible combinations of these categories. To help identify some of the possibilities for a selected topic, three charts have been constructed: tables 2, 3, and 4.

TABLE 2 / Combining the Concrete and the Abstract

	Process	Problem	Value
Person	Richard Nixon and the introduction of P.P.B.S. budgeting	Gen. Lewis Hershey and the alienation of American youth	Will Rogers and the development of American political satire
Event	The election of 1928 and the growth of the New Deal coalition	The Treaty of Versailles and the rise of Adolf Hitler	The War of 1812 and the tradition of political dissent
Entity	The Sierra Club and the mobilization of public opinion on conservation	The Irish Republican Army (IRA) and violence in Northern Ireland	The Anti-Federalists and the development of the idea of citizen participation in administration
Law or Policy	Aid to Latin America and the congressional appropriations process	The first amendment and the problem of obscenity in the mail	FHA and the development of the idea of a "stake in society"
Object	Techniques that Impressionist painters use in order to communicate their world view	How an audience can derive meaning from an abstract painting like Mondrian's "Broadway Boogie Woogie"	Frank Lloyd Wright's "Falling Waters" and the development of organic architecture

Specific Purpose and Thesis

The direction that these combinations take depends, of course on the general purpose of the speaker. To select a focused central idea for the speech, look at table 1 again. The items in the left hand column marked "Specific Purpose and Thesis" have the function of giving the speech unity and focus. They also tell where the speaker plans to direct his topic and how he plans to treat it generally, with what approach and to what end.

The specific purpose and the thesis sentence, although different, are closely linked and so may be discussed together

TABLE 3 / Combining Two Abstractions as a Focus

	Process	*Problem*	*Value*
Process	The conflict between internal congressional and constituent pressures upon Congresswoman Shirley Chisholm	The election of federal judges and the problems of conflict of interest	The development of political attitudes in the comic strip "Peanuts"
Problem	Vice-presidential press relations: the problem of Spiro Agnew	Organized crime, wiretapping, and the right of privacy	Rational choice in presidential elections and the threat of television image-making
Value	The impact of capital punishment on prison discipline	Adam Clayton Powell, and the right of Congress to expel its members	Guerilla theater versus presentational theater

here. A specific purpose deals with the response that a speaker wishes to receive from his audience. For instance, a specific purpose for the topic in table 2 that combines entity and problem may be written like this: "To inform my audience about the Irish Republican Army's responsibility for violence in Northern Ireland."

A thesis deals with the ideas utilized in order to accomplish the specific purpose. Topics, such as those found in tables 2, 3, and 4, are combined with ideas or stances concerning them. The result should be a complete declarative sentence that states the main idea of the speech. It should provide good, clear reasons for including the information found in the body of the speech, as well as good reasons for excluding other information. The topic in table 2 that combines entity and problem, for example, might be transformed into a thesis merely by changing it to state, "The Irish Republican Army (IRA) is responsible for [creating] violence in Northern Ireland." This would be appropriate to the general purpose of being informative. In order to follow the general purpose to persuade, a specific purpose such

TABLE 4 / Combining Concrete Objects of Study on the Basis of an Abstraction

	Person	Event	Entity	Law or Policy	Object
Person	Tennessee Williams and Arthur Miller: a comparison of two realistic playwrights	George McGovern and the Democratic Convention of 1972	George Wallace and his impact on organized labor	U Thant and the development of U.N. police action	Michelangelo and his Sistine Chapel ceiling frescoes
Event	Mayor Richard Daley and the election of John F. Kennedy in 1960	A comparison of two campaigns: Henry Wallace 1948, George Wallace 1968	The A.M.A. and defeat of Medicare in 1961	The Farmers' Holiday and the growth of agricultural price supports	The Eiffel Tower and the Paris Exposition of 1889
Entity	Robert McNamara and the reorganization of the Department of Defense	The American Legion and the Viet Nam War	Kenya and Tanzania: a comparison of electoral process	The Office of Passports and Communist Cuba	The Latin Cross and its significance in the Christian Church
Law or Policy	Secretary of Interior Udall and the development of the new conservation	The Open Housing Law and the election of Ronald Reagan as Governor of California	The Neighborhood Legal Service and the city government of Chicago	Two approaches to rural poverty: Department of Agriculture and the Office of Economic Opportunity	The rack and other instruments of torture and James I's anti-witchcraft statute of 1604
Object	Rembrandt's self-portraits	The floor plan of a basilica and a Catholic church service	The round table and the organization and philosophy of King Arthur's court	The signet ring and royal decree	Andy Warhol's "tomato soup" paintings and "cartoon" paintings: how they reflect the spirit of the 20th century

as the following could be written: "To persuade my audience that Americans should stop giving monetary aid to the Irish Republican Army." The thesis sentence could then read like this: "The Irish Republican Army is responsible for [creating] violence in Northern Ireland, therefore Americans should refuse to give them monetary aid."

Each thesis has several important characteristics. It must be *properly narrowed* so that a speaker can qualify and support his generalizations in the time allotted. A thesis such as, "The IRA is both good and bad for the people of Northern Ireland," might be an example of a broad idea that could not be properly covered in a reasonable length of time. A thesis must also be *unified* and speak about one thing, class of things, or idea. The following sample thesis would be considered disunified: "The IRA's techniques are ineffective in gaining freedom for the people of Northern Ireland and their treatment of girls who become engaged to British soldiers is unjust and inhumane." A thesis must be *concretely worded.* It should not be a broad statement, such as, "Several organizations in the world are responsible for a majority of the world's violence." It is preferable to be more specific and to talk about the Irish Republican Army in Northern Ireland, for example, rather than "several" organizations from unspecified areas of the globe. Words or phrases such as "few," "several," "many," "many different," "much," "varying," "factors," "some," "diverse," and "various" should alert the speaker that he is trying to cover too much ground or, to put it another way, that he has not properly narrowed his topic.

If a thesis is clearly argumentative, it should be truly debatable. For example, most people would agree that poverty should be eliminated. Controversy enters when methods for eliminating it are suggested. Theses of speeches to persuade and to activate should have the form of a simple declarative sentence. Questions may be used to unify and focus discussions and debates. The language of all theses should be unslanted and objective. Avoid inflammatory statements such as, "Only Texas oil-millionaires and other filthy capitalists are against eradicating poverty."

Both specific purposes and theses are difficult to write because most of the research must be completed before they can be clearly expressed. Considerable time and thought should go into their preparation since they reflect the speaker's knowledge and insight.

RESEARCHING THE SPEECH

A rough outline can be prepared on the basis of a preliminary survey of the topic. An outline ideally is divided into from two to five main headings. These headings enumerate the various parts of the topic to be investigated. This initial outline is a guide for research. An outline is a skeleton to which material may be added or from which it can be removed when the final draft is prepared. There are several reasons for constructing this outline, none of which is based on the whim of the instructor. The main reason is that it insures clear thinking and provides guidelines for all subsequent research.

The next step is to gather the needed information. The speaker will find the books, pamphlets, magazines, journals, and newspapers he needs; or interview experts in the field. The best point of departure in preparing a bibliography (a list of sources used), is to utilize the bibliographies appearing in class textbooks. Using material from a class that applies to a speech will not only give the speaker added confidence, but should also increase his knowledge in the subject area. He should then check the library to see if those sources are available. This is done by examining the card catalogue files kept by all libraries listing the books in the collection. The files are alphabetized by authors, subjects, and titles with all books listed in each.

Periodicals can be covered through the indexes and abstracts that are kept up-to-date by librarians. Indexes (not those found at the back of books that list items found in those books, but a separate volume) list information such as where and when the article was published. Abstracts give this information plus a brief resume of the article's contents. These references are arranged by author, title, subject, or a combination of all three. Examples of such indexes are *Reader's Guide* to *Periodical Literature, Public Affairs Information Service Index, Humanities and Social Science Index,* and *The New York Times Index.* These and other valuable sources are discussed in Part II. Since these sources refer to journals and magazine articles rather than published book-length treatments, they are often the sources of the freshest material.

Should the topic selected be what is known by journalists as a breaking story—that is an ongoing and still developing topic—then the student may find materials published by the federal government or by the United Nations of invaluable help. Whatever the case, whatever the nature of the topic, there is a vast supply of books, magazines, pamphlets, tracts, and other relevant documents available to add depth and direction to scholarly research.

Bibliography Cards

The best and easiest way to prepare a bibliography is to use 4 X 6 or 5 X 8 index cards, lined or unlined, on which to note the pertinent data. On these the name of the author, title of the book, the edition, the publisher's names, place of publication, date of publication, and volume number are written.

If the material is contained in a journal, the necessary data includes the author, title of the article, name of the journal, volume number, date of publication, and the page numbers of the article. In either case, the library classification number should be added so that if the material needs to be rechecked, it can be easily located. A separate card, of course, should be used for each source and, later on, each idea or quotation. In the latter case, note the source in an abbreviated form with the appropriate page references.

Checking the Bibliography

Once the bibliography is compiled, it becomes urgent to determine if the volumes and journals listed are, indeed, available in the library. And if they are, then the student must scan them to be sure that they do contain material relevant to the topic.

Using the library classification numbers, the student can go directly to the shelf where a check of the chapter contents or the index of a volume will show if it can be of use. If the book appears useful, a notation on the index card should explain in what way it can be used.

Taking Notes

Now the material gathered by the student must be read and from it all pertinent information extracted. The resultant research notes should be transcribed clearly and concisely on index cards, each card marked with the title of the source and page reference. A key phrase at a top corner is used to describe the subject matter on the notecard. Putting only one type of information on each card makes it easier to rearrange them, and so help in the final sessions of organization.

When an author is paraphrased, or restated in a student's own words, care should be taken to insure that his intent is not distorted. Direct quotations must be exact. Notes generally should be as brief as is practical, but if they run long, the student should number each card used in sequence.

The Library Card Catalog

Practically every library in the United States uses one of two classification systems—the Dewey decimal classification or the Library of Congress classification. These two classification systems differ in their approach; an explanation of each follows.

DEWEY DECIMAL CLASSIFICATION

Melvil Dewey worked out this approach in the latter part of the nineteenth century. The Dewey decimal classification system divides all knowledge, as represented by books and other materials that are acquired by libraries, into nine main classes which are numbered by digits 1 to 9. Material too general to belong to any one of these classes, such as newspapers and encyclopedias, falls into a tenth class, numbered 0, which precedes the others. The classes are written as hundreds; thus, 000 is general works, 100 is philosophy, 200 is religion, 300 social sciences, and so on. Each division is again divided into nine sections preceded by a general section; thus, 800 is literature in general, while speech is a subdivision in the 808 section. Divisions to bring together similar materials are made by the addition of digits following a decimal point. Usually, most numbers do not exceed six digits in length, i.e., three to the right of the decimal point; however, there are cases of numbers extending to nine and sometimes even more digits.

The basic classification system ranges from 000 to 999:

000-099 General works
100-199 Philosophy

200-299   Religion
300-399   Social sciences
400-499   Language
500-599   Pure sciences
600-699   Technology
700-799   Arts
800-899   Literature
900-999   History

Of most relevance to students in the field of speech are the items in 800-899.

800-809   Miscellaneous: history, criticism, composition, etc.
810-819   American (U.S.) literature
820-829   English literature
830-839   German literature
840-849   French literature
850-859   Italian literature
860-869   Spanish literature
870-879   Latin literature
880-889   Greek literature
890-899   Literature of other languages

800-809 is broken down into ten subclasses, each of which may be further subdivided by the use of decimals.

801   Philosophy and theory
802   Handbooks and outlines
803   Dictionaries and encyclopedias
804   Essays and lectures
805   Periodicals
806   Organizations and societies
807   Study and teaching
808   Literary composition
809   History and criticism of literature

The very specific spot designated to speech is the 808 section.

808.1   Poetry
808.2   Drama
808.3   Fiction
808.4   Essays
808.5   Speech and public speaking

808.51   Public speaking (oratory)
808.52   Voice, expression, gesture
808.53   Debating
808.54   Recitation techniques (storytelling, reading aloud)
808.55   Choral speaking
808.56   Conversation
808.6   Letters
808.7   Satire and humor
808.8   Collections from several literatures
808.9   Literatures of artificial languages

For the complete list of subclassifications see the *Dewey Decimal Classification and Relative Index,* 18th ed., 2 vols. New York: Forest Press, Inc., of Lake Placid Club Education Foundation, 1970.

LIBRARY OF CONGRESS CLASSIFICATION

The Library of Congress classification system was adopted in 1900, three years after the Library of Congress moved from the capitol to its new building. It changed systems in order to have a more systematic and functional arrangement of the Library's collection.

This system divided the fields of knowledge into twenty groups by assigning a letter to each and combining arabic numerals and additional letters to separate the main groups into classes and subclasses in somewhat of a similar way used in the Dewey decimal system. All books are divided into the following basic groups:

A	General works	H	Social science
B	Philosophy and religion	J	Political Science
C	History and auxiliary sciences	K	Law
		L	Education
D	Foreign history and topography	M	Music
		N	Fine arts
E-F	American history	P	Language and literature
G	Geography and anthropology	Q	Science
		R	Medicine

S	Agriculture	**V**	Naval science
T	Technology	**Z**	Bibliography and library
U	Military science		science

For students in the field of speech, class P (language and literature) is the most relevant. Within each class subdivisions are denoted by a second letter. Thus for Literature and language, we have the following subclasses:

P	Philology and linguistics (Gen.)
PA	Classical languages and literatures
PB-PH	Modern European languages
PJ-PL	Oriental languages and literature
PM	Hyperborean, American and artificial languages
PN	Literary history and collections (Gen.)
PQ	Romance literature
PR	English literature
PS	American literature
PT	Teutonic literature
PZ	Short stories and juvenile literature

Within this structure, the specific area that applies to speech and includes all aspects of oratory, oral interpretation of literature, and debate is PN4000-4600. Anything having to do with radio is found in the division TK6540-6570, with broadcasting being in the TK6570.B7 subdivision. Information concerning television is found in the following areas: HE8690-8699 and TK6630. Television production and direction may be found in PN1991.75, while television broadcasting is found in the GV880 section. Each subclass makes up several smaller regional, historical, or functional subdivisions. For the complete list of subsclassifications see Classification: Classes PN, TK, HE and GV, and see the appropriate volumes from the following publication: *Classification.* Washington: Library of Congress Processing Department, Subject Cataloging Division, 1966.

Putting It All Together

ORGANIZATION AND OUTLINING

When the original material has been read and all relevant items are on index cards, they can be organized by the student. He should read the notes carefully. This helps to provide a comprehensive overview of the material. It also provides insight into which materials support and which contradict his thesis. Next, using the rough draft of his outline as a guide, he should begin mentally building the speech from the information he has amassed.

At this point the student may decide his material indicates that a new or different tack should be taken, that it is advisable to alter the original outline, perhaps drastically, or that he was on target right from the start. Whatever the decision, a final outline may now be made—the one on which the researched facts must ultimately hang.

Form is the pattern or organization that helps to communicate the ideas in a speech to the listener. It is imperative to use strategy by choosing the form that will most likely suit the general and the specific purposes of the speech. Table 1 refers to the various types of organizations that pertain to the four general purposes. The chart then notes the strategy as it involves the delivery, the speaker, the occasion, and the audience. For instance, a speaker may wish to use the organization of admissions and concessions (p. 23), because admitting that the opposition has some truth on its side lets the audience know that the speaker is not narrow-minded and that he has thoroughly studied the problem. They may then be more willing to listen to the arguments and be persuaded by them.

General Outlining Rules

Whatever form is used, it must be clearcut to the speaker and the audience or confusion will result. The major job of the outline is to promote clear thinking. General rules basic to all good outlines are listed here.

1. Adopt an outlining system and be consistent in its use. The generally accepted form consists of the following pattern of letters, numbers, and indentations:
     I.
        A.
        B.
           1.
           2.
              a.
              b.
2. The thesis will generally be clearly and sufficiently supported if a strict hierarchy is adhered to. The Roman numerals, as major breakdowns, should clearly and directly support the thesis. The capital letters should clearly support the Roman numeral under which they are placed. The Arabic numerals should clearly support the one capital letter under which they are placed and the small letters should clearly support the Arabic numeral under which they are placed. If relationships are foggy, it could mean that one's thinking is foggy, or that the headings should be reworded rather than discarded.
3. To insure clear thinking, each heading should be written in the form of a simple declarative sentence.
4. To enhance consistency, each group of headings directly related (such as all of the Roman numerals, all the capital letters supporting one Roman numeral, etc.) should be written in parallel structure. (see also p. 37) Beginning each of these groups with the same word would help achieve this goal.

5. Subject matter should not overlap in the headings.
6. If subheadings are used, there should be at least two. When something is divided there must be at least two pieces. If there is only one, not much thought has been expended on the area.

Speech Outlines

Speech outlines, specifically, should have between two and five main headings. The ideal is either two or three because listeners can absorb only so many ideas. They cannot turn back a page to recall what has been said. Here is an organizational pattern for the speech outline. The body of the speech will follow the general rules listed above. Since the introduction and conclusion do not always lend themselves to division into idea units, they cannot invariably be outlined. Each of the sections shown below should be clearly labeled on the outline.

General Purpose

Specific Purpose and/or Thesis

Introduction to Speech Body

I.
  A.
  B.
II.
  A.
  B.

Conclusion of Speech

(Bibliography—to submit if necessary)

Patterns of Organization

Depending upon the purpose and the material, a speaker should be aware of many specific types of organization.

INTRODUCTIONS
Introductions, for instance, have a basic pattern. Whether the purpose is to inform, entertain, persuade, or activate, they must

begin with an *attention step* to catch the audience's interest. Many different techniques may be used to accomplish this. They are dealt with in the preceding section and also are referred to in the third column of table 1. After the attention step comes the *need step.* This is important for all types of speeches because the audience must know why they should listen to the speech and why it is timely or important to them. Next should come a clear *statement of the purpose or thesis,* so that the audience does not have to guess about the speaker's intentions. This will help them be more discriminating when listening to the development of the central idea. A *statement of the outline* may, but does not always, follow the statement of the purpose. However, it is a great aid to comprehension and clarification.

THE BODY OF THE SPEECH

Patterns of organization used in the body of the speech help both to inform and entertain the audience. The *spatial pattern* helps to clarify a physical area that is being discussed, such as the layout of a church interior. A *chronological pattern* is used to explain a process or progression. It is frequently used in "how-to-do-it" speeches, for narratives (as of travels), or when historical periods or biographies are being described. For instance, a speaker wishing to describe the artistic development of Picasso would divide his speech into major headings that covered his youngest years, his "blue period", Cubism, collage, and so on.

One of the most popular types of organization, the *topical pattern,* is useful when breaking a thesis down to its component parts. Some subjects, such as major divisions of the United States government, may be naturally split up. Other areas may not break down as obviously as this, or the speaker may not be able to include all of the natural divisions of an area in the time allotted to him. For example, anthropologists' have studied many aspects of witchcraft including herbal cures, love potions, curses, associations with the devil, belief in fertility, rituals, holidays, astral travel, methods of divination, belief in reincarnation, and the spirit world. The trick to making a good thesis out of this wealth of material is to choose two or three (depending upon how much time you have) of the aspects that are the most closely related and ignore the rest. "The witches' love of life may be seen in their emphasis on fertility and in their use of herbs to cure the sick" is a thesis sentence that can be arrived at in this manner. The main headings of the outline would then be the following:

I. The witches' love of life may be seen in their emphasis on fertility.
II. The witches' love of life may be seen in their use of herbs to cure the sick.

The *causal pattern* of organization is useful because it helps the audience to know why something happened. Obviously, it is especially important when dealing with subjects such as natural laws or phenomena in the area of the natural and social sciences. Since an effect may have more than one cause, these naturally should be enumerated. If, for example, the topic was President Nixon's landslide reelection in 1972, one might discuss Dr. Henry Kissinger's announcement of the forthcoming peace in Vietnam on October 25, 1972, as well as other causal factors such as the disarray of the Democratic forces, and so forth.

The *purpose-means pattern* is especially useful when dealing with processes or arts. In the first part of the speech body the purpose will be presented and discussed, and in the second part the practical means of operation, etc., are analyzed. A speaker may thus discuss the theme of a work of art and then go on to describe the techniques that were used by the artist to communicate this theme.

For the *question pattern,* main headings of the outline should be statements made in response to questions. This organization anticipates questions that the audience members might ask about a certain subject. If one were arguing the case for abortion, the main headings could be stated like this:

I. Legalized abortion should not be considered murder.
II. Legalized abortion will not cause an increased decline in morality.

III. Legalized abortion will not cause women to be subjected to physical danger.

IV. Legalized abortion will not cause a continued drain on hospital facilities.

While several of these types of organizations may be used for speeches of all general purposes, the organizations most often used for the purposes of persuasion or activation include the following patterns: classical, problem-solution, expository, theory-practice, desirable-practicable, deduction, induction, general statement-to-typical example, comparison, contrast, refutation, admissions and concessions, and propositional. The *classical pattern* runs as follows: attention step; narration (background information and other explanatory material); an outline of the points to be proved; the proof, refutation or opposition to arguments against the approach; and the summary and appeal step. It is used when a full discussion of the proposition is desired and can be used as a model for more restrictive speeches.

The *problem-solution pattern* is useful when the speaker is aware of a problem, when he wishes to make his audience aware and concerned, and when he wants the audience to accept his solution and possibly to make them wish to help him put his plan into operation. To be an effective organizational pattern, there must be evidence of a real problem. All the causes of the problem must be covered, otherwise the speaker cannot prove that his solution will solve it. The following is an example of a stock *problem-solution* outline:

I. Attention Step

II. This was the *problem*
    A. Importance of
    B. Nature of
    C. Causes of

III. This solution solved   *or*   III. This program should
the problem   be adopted
    A. Nature of   A. Nature of
    B. How solution   B. It will solve the
       solved problem   problem

C. Estimation of
total results
IV. Appeal Step

C. Why it is best
one available
D. It will not create
additional prob-
lems that are as
bad as or worse
than the original.

The *expository pattern* is laid out in the manner of a traditional informative speech with the purpose at the beginning and the proof laid out with an appearance of being merely informative. It takes extra work because an outline for a clearly persuasive speech should be made first, then the expository outline will be based in part on it. Because its tone is that of a reporter or scientist instead of a pleader, an especially hostile or uninformed audience may respond favorably to it.

The *theory-practice* and *desirable-practicable* patterns are nearly the same. The first section of the speech body deals with a situation as it should ideally be—or be handled ideally—and the second part deals with the real and existing situation, or the situation as it can be handled practically in real life.

Deduction is a form of logic that draws relationships between a known, accepted principle (major premise) and the immediate specific problem (minor premise). Similarities between the two situations are drawn and then a conclusion based upon the comparison is given. For instance, a man sees a girl walking by wearing a short, quilted jacket; a knitted cap and scarf; tight dark trousers covered with snow; and heavy boots and gloves. He deduces from her outfit and the snow on it that she is a skier. His deduction may be confirmed when he sees her later with a pair of skis over her shoulder. For speech-making, the deduction pattern is most effective if the audience can accept the major premise easily. The minor premise will then receive support. There must be sufficient, reliable evidence to support the premise—exceptional cases must not weaken the generalization—and the meanings of the premises should be clearly related to each other. A general pattern for deductive organization is as follows:

   I.   General Conclusion
      A.   Major Premise
      B.   Minor (specific) Premise

Some specialized work in logic will be necessary before the student can work well with this type of organization—or even with induction. Recommended books in the study of logic are found on page 140.

Induction, however, is less complicated than deduction and, on looking back at the skiing example, one will see that it even makes up a part of deduction by providing supporting evidence to the two premises. Its form can be compared to the type of detective story that leads toward the guilty party slowly—clue by clue, detail by detail. A footprint or fingerprint here, a piece of dirt there, added to a candy wrapper or cigarette butt, draw the reader into the mystery and lead both him and the detective to the same conclusion. This form is used in a speech when people are unconcerned or do not want to admit there is a problem. They would be turned off if they were immediately confronted with the purpose or proposition, so the proof in the form of specific details is presented first and the conclusion or major generalization last. Facts must be organized to imply the need without stating it directly. In short speeches the conclusion need not be stated plainly, since audiences do enjoy drawing their own conclusions.

The *general statement to typical example pattern,* which is often based upon only one major illustration, is especially effective for short speeches. The typical example will need the most defense; and, since a variety of illustrations are not being used, the delivery and style should be particularly vivid.

The *comparative pattern* is used if there is a desire to analyze two or more things at one time in order to show similarities. Dissimilarities must not overshadow the similarities. Here is an example of one way a comparative pattern may be organized:

   I.   This solution would work in my situation
      A.   It works in this other situation
      B.   My situation is similar to this other situation

Organization may also follow either the block-by-block or the point-by-point system. A speaker may wish to prove, for example, that the play *Camino Real* by the American playwright Tennessee Williams is similar to *A Dream Play* by the Swedish playwright August Strindberg. Using the block-by-block system, Williams' play might be discussed first, then Strindberg's. The point-by-point system would cover the individual points of comparison, such as the themes, the character types, and the imagery in the two plays. The organization of the *contrast pattern* is nearly the same as that of the *comparison* except that now the speaker wishes to analyze two or more things or ideas in order to show their differences. Of course, there would be no object in doing this unless there were also some major similarities present that would justify the contrast.

In the *refutation pattern,* the opposition's point of view is presented first and then reasons for objections to that point of view are given. The reason for including the opposition's point of view is to refute it. Well-informed audiences respond well if both sides of an issue are presented. The audience usually has arguments of its own and if the speaker does not cover them, he cannot refute them and therefore cannot persuade or convince the audience. It is important to convince the audiences that one has considered all the evidence. The closely related *admissions and concessions pattern* consists of admitting that the opposition has some truth on its side and then presenting the point of contention to be discussed and expanded. The concession must not weaken the speaker's main argument so it is placed in a subordinate position while the speaker's point is placed in a climactic position where there is room for expansion. For instance, it may be conceded that the space program used money that could help the poverty-stricken in the ghettoes; however, it did provide jobs for many people and increased the nation's wealth and its knowledge of life on other planets. This approach keeps the audience from thinking that the problem was not studied thoroughly. It makes the speaker's position seem more significant and leaves the audience with the speaker's ideas, which makes the speech more persuasive.

A *propositional organization* presents the solution first and then supplies the support or proof for the proposition. A major proposition may thus state that more teachers' colleges should diversify their programs and add more vocational courses. Decreased student enrollment, unemployment in the teaching ranks, and an increased demand for such vocations as policemen and nurses may be used to support the contention. Normally speaking, the climactic order (most important argument or proof placed last) is most effective because it enhances tension and, therefore, attention.

CONCLUSIONS

The conclusion of a speech should aid in comprehension and retention. (In order to do this, a general summary of what has been said in the speech may be made, If the speech has been quite lengthy, the major points may be listed or restated. The conclusion should also let the audience know that the speech is ending and should leave them with a good impression. The best way to do this is to utilize one of the most appropriate techniques, which will be discussed in the next section, and to also use a variety of transitional techniques in getting to the conclusion. Do not be satisfied with merely saying, "In conclusion . . . ." This is your last chance to drive home the point of the speech, so if the desire is to persuade or activate, the strongest plea will be placed in the conclusion.

STYLE

The next major step in speech preparation, after doing the research and organizing it, is to compose the speech and thus determine its style. This may involve writing it or merely thinking about it and rehearsing aloud. If this step is omitted, the speaker may end up stuttering and stammering instead of appearing articulate and knowledgeable.

In this manual "style" is defined as the usage of specific words, images, and sentence constructions, and does not include the overall organization in its scope. Major aspects of style are listed to the right of the section labeled "style" in table 1. Since this does not purport to be an in-depth study, a speech student should refer to specialized style manuals some of which are listed on page 90.

Word Choice

Wording should be as brief, concrete, and precise as possible so that meanings cannot be misconstrued. Words should not be used merely to impress the audience. Depending upon the level of formality, there is a choice of three major language classifications: 1) literary or formal, 2) common—which, though it is more relaxed grammatically, may be used for most occasions, and 3) colloquial or vulgate, which is ungrammatical and may include "four-letter" words. These classifications may be modified, depending upon the audience. In order to keep the audience's attention, there should be a variety of word choice. Repeat only significant words.

Variety and vividness may be achieved through the use of imagery. Some types of imagery include the simile, metaphor, personification, metonymy, hyperbole, understatement, and irony. *Similes* and *metaphors* are types of comparisons. The difference is that a simile includes the words "like" or "as"—i.e. "Her eyes were like stars"—while the metaphor does not—i.e. "her eyes were stars." *Personifications* give human qualities to abstractions or inanimate objects: "Spring gracefully dances across the lawn." A *metonymy* involves the substitution of a term closely associated with a word for the word itself. Thus "the crown" may stand for "king" or "rosy fingers" may stand for the whole child. A *hyperbole* is a type of exaggeration that stresses the importance of something. A woman saying, "Everybody just adored my new suit," probably just meant that a couple of people said her outfit looked attractive. An *understatement* is the opposite of a hyperbole. A speaker can create humor by saying something like, "Aristotle Onassis has done rather well in the shipping business." *Irony,* produced by implying the opposite of what is said can become quite complex because many people tend to take all statements literally; therefore, a speaker must be sure that his voice inflections and facial expression convey the idea. One of the better known examples of irony occurred when Shakespeare's Mark Antony called Brutus an "honorable man." *Sarcasm and satire,* closely related to irony, present the ridiculous aspects of an idea, person, etc., yet differ in the speaker's attitude toward his subject—satire being the more objective, witty and urbane; and sarcasm intending to wound more than to correct. Using several of these types of imagery in a speech will help make it more vivid and interesting.

Sentence Structure

Sentence structure can also aid in providing variety and interest. Its syntax can be arranged into three basic types: 1) simple, 2) compound, 3) complex. The *simple sentence* has a subject and verb, in that order, and may or may not have other parts, such as prepositional phrases, objects, predicate nouns, etc.: "Jane ran." A *compound sentence* consists of two simple sentences connected by a conjunction such as "and" or "but"—"Jane ran and Sally walked." If the conjunction can be substituted for a period, resulting in two complete simple sentences, the sentence is compound. However, if only one part of the sentence can stand alone and one part cannot, but still contains a subject and verb, the sentence is *complex* and consists of an independent and a dependent clause—"Jane ran when the dog chased her." A *compound-complex sentence* will be formed if the sentence includes two or more independent clauses and one or more dependent clauses: "While the dog barked and growled, Jane ran and Sally walked down the dusty road."

These major sentence arrangements can be altered even more. They may have just the *subject-verb pattern*—"Sally walked down the road." They may have the *subject-verb-object pattern*—"Dick dropped the ball." Or they may have a *subject-verb-nominative pattern*—"Dick is a poor athlete." An inverted sentence may be created by placing the verb before the subject —"Down the road walked Sally." Placement of adjectives and adverbs and their phrases and clauses may vary. Emphasis may be altered through the use of *coordination* or *subordination* of the idea in a sentence. Coordination implies a balancing of equal

parts. Good coordination shows a clear and meaningful relationship between parts, as can be seen in the following two examples. The second one illustrates the clearer relationship:

1. Henry was standing on the corner eating a candy bar
   and an old man came up to ask him for a dime.
2. Henry was standing on the corner eating a candy bar
   when an old man came up to ask him for a dime.

Parallelism is a type of coordination that makes two elements of a sentence equal in emphasis and importance—"The
young girl clutched the piece of ice and rushed into the kitch-
en." In most instances, subordination is a way to give secondary
emphasis to an idea, even though it may be an important fact.
Usually a speaker places his most important idea in the main
clause. In the following examples the first sentence emphasizes
the idea of the girl rushing into the kitchen. The second sentence emphasizes the fact that she is clutching some ice.

1. Clutching a slippery piece of ice, the young girl rushed
   into the kitchen.
2. Rushing into the kitchen, the young girl clutched a
   piece of slippery ice.

Sentences may be long or short. Placing a short sentence in
the midst of longer ones will tend to emphasize it, so it should
contain or direct attention to the most important idea. Placing
the independent clause at the end of a sentence will create
tension and emphasize it. For example—"Rushing and stum-
bling along, nearly blinded by terror, yet attempting to maintain her sense of direction, Allison made her way through the
forest." Introducing sentences that ask questions, exclaim, or
command will also help create variety. All of these techniques
not only make speeches more interesting, but also increase
comprehension.

Twenty Speech Techniques

Every speech is improved through the use of a number of
different techniques. This list describes the most important of
them.

1. A *rhetorical question* to which no response is required helps to set the stage for subsequent information.
2. A *direct question* that the audience actually is expected to answer may be used also. However, this device poses a much larger threat than does a rhetorical question where no verbal answer is expected. It is possible to woo the audience by choosing questions to which it will nod rather than respond in words.
3. *Humor* should be sprinkled throughout most speeches, even though the topic may be serious. It catches the audience's attention and regenerates its interest. Since it also soothes tension, it is especially effective with a hostile audience. Be sure the jokes are relevant to the subject and that they are neither old nor crude. Being able to understand incongruities and timing will help in the use of humor.
4. *Stories* provide excitement, drama, and pathos. They build up suspense, which in turn builds audience interest. Additional human interest and credibility is created if the stories are true and if they describe something that the speaker himself has experienced. Stories should be short, to the point, and relate to the main idea of the speech.
5. *Illustrations* differ from stories in that they do not build to a climax or contain elements of suspense. They will be more interesting and persuasive if the speaker uses himself as a basic source as much as possible. In order to be really convincing, the speaker needs enough of these illustrations to warrant the conclusion; but they must be vital, meaningful, true, and typical.
6. *Hypothetical situations* are used when the speaker cannot find real or factual examples. They are less effective than the "real" illustration or example because people tend to believe and pay more attention to what is real.
7. *Quotations* should be short, fresh, striking and truly fit the subject. They add interest and believability

because of their authoritativeness, but the audience must respect and esteem the authority. State the source first so that the audience can evaluate the quote. The authority should be unprejudiced, well known, acceptable to the audience, and accurately quoted by the speaker. His ideas should also be corroborated by other authorities. Poetry or prose fiction may be used as well as quotes from "authorities." When delivering quotations, the most effective technique is to glance down at the notes, but deliver them when looking up. Credit should also be given when *testimony* is used as a technique. Most of the discussion concerning quotations would apply here, because testimony differs from a quote only in that the exact words of the source are not used. Ideas are paraphrased.

8. *Startling statements of fact* may be used as a technique, especially in the introduction, to catch the audience's attention.

9. *Plain statements of fact, statistics,* or *quantification* are the best types of proof that a speaker can use. New or unusual ones that the audience has not heard before are especially effective. Choose the latest and best data, but do not include too many or the audience will become bored. Double-check sources for accuracy and do not rely on only one source. Be aware of fallacies in the use of statistics.

10. *Analogies* show a parallel between two things that were thought to be unrelated to each other. They may be used to make a subject or idea more meaningful or more intellectually interesting to an audience. It takes analytical insight to refute them, so they do make good support material. It is important, however, to identify with the audience in order to choose effective ones. They should be plausible, and not trite. "Black as sin" is an example of a trite analogy.

11. *Contrast* shows differences in basically similar things. An idea or object becomes more vivid and dramatic

when seen in juxtaposition with ones that differ greatly.

12. *Examples* aid in clarification and believability, especially if they are real and not hypothetical. They should be concrete and should contain enough details to provide substantial support. Names and dates should be included whenever possible.

13. *History of the question* is the technique used to establish the need issue, or to help support the idea that there really is a problem to be solved. It also provides background information necessary for the comprehension of an idea or problem. Terms that are central to the meaning of the speech or technical terms may need to be defined. For greatest effect, terms should be defined immediately after being used, and those terms that need definition should be kept to a minimum.

14. *Reasoning* as a technique requires a calm, intelligent approach that is more effective than an emotional delivery. Basically it includes the use of *induction* or *deduction* (see pp. 31-32). There should be a combination of specific evidence, inference, and a conclusion. Support is needed to prove that the specific evidence was typical. It is sometimes a good idea to acknowledge that there may be reservations or exceptions.

15. *Specific reference* is one technique that should catch the audience's attention. The speaker may refer to a number of things including himself, the group, the occasion, a specific individual, another speaker, something familiar to the audience, or to the significance of the subject. Derogatory references may alienate an audience, so they should be avoided or at least carefully handled.

16. *Compliments* aimed at the audience should be sincere. This will result in making the speaker more acceptable to the audience, and so more receptive to his message.

17. *Self-identification* is another technique that enhances audience trust. If the speaker is well known, he may not need to state his qualifications and background, or

he may have the difficult problem of altering his image. In any event, this technique will help him do it.

18. *Repetition* or restatement is particularly important when an idea needs to be emphasized. It aids comprehension and retention, but may get boring if used indiscriminately.

19. *Imagery* (see pp. 35) can be a great aid to comprehension if it is handled with care. It is a delicate matter, and the speaker must have a close identification with his audience to use it effectively.

20. *Novel techniques,* which may be entirely unique or may be a different combination of the previously mentioned techniques, can add freshness and zest to the speech. They are most usually found in introductions as attention-getting devices.

Fallacies in Logic to Avoid

If a speaker is to be convincing, he must speak logically. He must be able to recognize such fallacies in his logic or reasoning as insufficient evidence; unreasonable extrapolation; the *non sequitur*; *post hoc, ergo propter hoc*; the distorted example; ignored effects; the red herring; the circular argument; and begging the question.

An argument may be controversial if there is *insufficient evidence* to convince everyone of its truth. That is, a speaker must give enough essential and specific support to convince an audience that the contentions are valid and are founded in reality.

Extrapolation is a surmise based on past events that suggests certain future courses of action. An *unreasonable extrapolation* is such a prediction that does not take all existing conditions into consideration, thereby rendering the prediction invalid.

Non sequitur is a Latin phrase that means "it does not follow." It occurs when too many steps and too much information have been omitted from an argument, causing a lack of relationship between supporting statements and the conclusion.

Literally meaning "after this, therefore because of this," the *post hoc, ergo propter hoc* is a special type of *non sequitur* argument having to do with cause-and-effect relationships. It is the assumption that one event was the cause of the other, which is many times difficult to support adequately. Another type of *non sequitur* is the *distorted example.* It is often used in deliberate efforts to deceive by using an example that does not prove what it claims to prove. For instance, low grades supposedly prove that a student is inferior in an area. The distortion arises from ignoring possibly important causes. The student may have been ill and unable to concentrate on his major exam; or the exam may have been deceptively worded, thereby causing him to use the wrong approach.

The *ignored effect* is a type of fallacy that occurs when the speaker does not consider the consequences of a proposed course of action that might cause more damage than the problem.

A *red herring* is an argument that diverts attention away from the central issue. Senator Joseph McCarthy was accused of using communism as a red herring for want of a better way to gain national attention. A speaker may also set up a *straw-man* to attack. The *straw-man* is a device for dwelling on minor, easily refuted points in order to avoid confronting the main issue. Usually it consists of attributing a position to an opponent that the opponent does not, in fact, hold, and then attacking that more easily demolished *straw-man* rather than the position the opponent actually holds.

The *circular argument* is often difficult to recognize since it uses itself to prove itself. Thus a speaker might support the claim that the Bible was written by God by reading quotations from the Bible. It is one form of the fallacy *begging the question,* by which the speaker asks the audience to accept a contention on a basis other than evidence. The truth of the argument is assumed without proving it. An example might be the argument stating that intelligent and informed people know smoking is hazardous to the health. People, because they wish to be thought intelligent and informed, are asked to accept the contention as true without the support of solid evidence, such as medical studies.

Using faulty reasoning in a speech can destroy the case one is trying to make. It is the responsibility of the speaker, and of the audience, to be able to recognize these common logical fallacies.

The Delivery

PREPARATION FOR DELIVERY

Speeches may be read, memorized, delivered extemporaneously, or given impromptu. Politicians or others afraid of being misquoted usually read their speeches and give copies of the manuscript to the press. Deliveries are smooth and formal, but audience rapport may be weak. A memorized speech usually improves each time it is given, but many times it sounds stilted because the speaker must concentrate on recalling his words rather than on emphasizing his ideas. It is difficult and time consuming to memorize a whole speech, and if a word is forgotten, the speaker may become lost. Extemporaneous speaking is most often emphasized in speech classes because it combines the best of the other forms of delivery. An extemporaneous speech is prepared ahead of time but delivered spontaneously. With the aid of a few notes consisting of key words indicating the outline, the speaker chooses his wording as he goes on. In this way, more of his personality is communicated to the audience. Care should be taken to use the heavy note cards, because sheets of paper rattle and are distracting. Write legibly on one side of the card to avoid confusion. Underline important ideas. Impromptu speaking requires no advance preparation; nevertheless, it is quite difficult to do well. The speaker must have a large fund of information, an organized mind, and practice in public speaking. The best way to be prepared for an impromptu speech is to be alert, keep up on current affairs, and then converse about them with friends. This will help you to formulate ideas in an organized, articulate manner.

DELIVERY

The best organized and the most effectively worded speech can, nevertheless, be a relative failure if it is not delivered well. There are two major aspects of delivery to be considered: the *vocal* aspect and the *physical* aspect. The vocal aspect consists of the voice in all its variations. The physical aspect is composed of facial and bodily gestures. These elements are all outlined in table 1 under the heading of "Delivery."

Vocal Aspect

The first rule of delivering an effective speech is that the audience must be able to hear it. The speaker must speak clearly. Each word must be enunciated audibly and pronounced according to standard usage. The speaker's voice helps to clarify his meaning, highlight his organization, and catch and hold the audience's attention. One does this by varying the pitch of the voice. Timing includes the rate of speech, which may be fast, slow, etc. Emphasis is gained by slowing down when covering a major point. A pause before and/or after a major idea will call it to the audience's attention. Repetitious vocal patterns that may be distracting should be avoided. Many people do not make the most use of their vocal mechanism because they are self-conscious and do not wish to reveal their feelings, or fear being deemed "theatrical." However, since both actors and speakers must keep the public interested over a long period of time, it might be well to cultivate a little more animation. Voice quality, which may be rough, breathy, clear, and so on, can both communicate and maintain audience interest. Voice tone is made up of all the vocal factors mentioned previously and can reveal the mood or a point of view that the speaker may not even wish to communicate to the audience.

Visual Aspect

The effective speaker has the audience's attention continuously. To accomplish this, the physical aspect is coordinated with the vocal aspect. The speaker must catch the audience's attention initially and keep recatching it throughout the course of the speech because an audience may be easily distracted. Facial expression will keep the audience's interest mainly through eye contact. Looking at even a few individuals in the audience will make many more think that a speaker is looking at them and their interest will be renewed because of the personal rapport created. Facial expression will also reveal enthusiasm or emotion and will communicate this to the audience, which will react accordingly. Movement of some kind guarantees either renewed interest or a distraction from speech content. Bodily gestures begin with a correct, relaxed posture and movement. But a speaker should move only with purpose or remain completely still, thereby avoiding distracting motions. The amount of movement must be appropriate to the motivation and enough to be expressive and hold interest.

Audio-Visual Aids

Audio-visual aids are used to attract and maintain attention, to increase comprehension, and to help the audience remember the speech better. They may also help a self-conscious speaker become more relaxed and natural. Various types of information can be communicated through pictures, cartoons, posters, maps, floor plans, charts, graphs, models, or diagrams. These may be presented through the mediums of overhead, slide, opaque, film-strip or motion-picture projectors; blackboards; mountings or drawings on paper or posterboard; or through a direct presentation. Three-dimensional objects may also be used. Audio aids, such as phonographs or tape recorders, may be found useful in presenting direct quotations spoken by their authors, literary quotations, background music, or musical illustrations.

All of these aids must be appropriate to the speech, the occasion, and the audience. They should complement, emphasize, or support contentions rather than call attention away from the ideas to themselves. If they are well prepared and smoothly presented, they will be effective. Since the audience must be able to understand them, they should be large, clear, simple, and neat. Using different vivid colors on charts, graphs, and similar materials will make them more legible and more interesting. Their complexity will be determined by the occasion and the audience's sophistication. Normally, small details should be omitted. If possible, material should not be displayed until it is time to discuss it. It should be positioned high enough for everyone to see. Hooks or clips above the blackboard, easels, tape, tacks, or hands may be used to hold them. Whichever method is used, it should not be distracting or clumsy. The speaker should stand to one side and be sure that neither he nor anything else is blocking the view. He should keep speaking while presenting the aid and speak to the audience, not to the aid, looking at it only when necessary. Use a pointer if possible, it will save dodging back and forth. When writing on a blackboard, the speaker should also direct most of his attention to the audience and keep talking while doing the work. He should read aloud written material that is presented by any visual aid. And, ideally, nothing should be passed around to the audience until the end of the speech, since this could prove distracting.

Preparation and practice are thus necessary in order to effectively utilize audio-visual aids. The speaker must not only know how to use all of the different types of phonographs, tape recorders, and projectors, but he must have them set up and ready to use. The sound should be comfortably adjusted, screens should be large enough for the image to be seen easily, rooms should be adequately dark for movies or projections, and the speaker must speak loudly enough to be heard over the projector noise. If possible, he should have someone else operate the projector in order not to place himself in a weak position behind the audience.

The overhead projector is probably the most effective of the audio-visual aids because the room does not need to be totally dark and the speaker may stand in front of the audience. While this projector cannot directly project flat objects such as pages of books, as can the opaque projector, its operation is noiseless. Tape recorders are smoother to use than phonographs because they are easy to start and stop, and the speaker does not have to hunt around for the right spot. All in all, audio-visual aids can contribute greatly to the effectiveness of a speech if they are adequately prepared and handled.

Bibliography and Footnotes

BIBLIOGRAPHY

The speaker usually composes a bibliography, since instructors and members of the audience may wish to examine sources. Speakers also may want to keep a list of sources for their own future reference. Some speakers place their bibliographical entries all together alphabetically by the authors' last names. For longer speeches it is helpful to divide them in categories such as books, periodicals, newspapers (sometimes combined with periodicals), government documents, dissertations, unpublished manuscripts, interviews, and letters. A bibliography should include all works cited in footnotes of a published speech plus any other works that were used. Works that were examined but not used should not be cited.

This section is included to give specific examples of the many different types of bibliographical entries that a speaker may need to make in the course of his career. First there is a list of general information essential to bibliographic entries of books and articles. Next are the main body of examples. Most of the forms offered here are based on *The University of Chicago Manual of Style,* 12th ed., rev. (Chicago: The University of Chicago Press, 1969). The manual does not, however, specifically cover several forms such as interviews and pamphlets, and in such cases, examples given are consistent with Kate L. Turabian's *Student Guide for Writing College Papers,* 2nd ed., rev. (Chicago: The University of Chicago Press, 1969).

General Rules

Book entries should include:

1. Full name of author(s), editors, or institutions responsible
2. Full title, including subtitle if one exists
3. Series, if any
4. Volume number
5. Editions, if not the original
6. City, publisher, and date of publication

Article entries should include:

1. Name of author
2. Title of article
3. Name of periodical
4. Volume number (or date, or both)
5. Pages

Specific Examples

Book With One Author

Bormann, Ernest G. *Theory and Research in the Communicative Arts.* New York: Holt, Rinehart and Winston, Inc., 1965.

Book With Two Authors

Scott, Robert L., and Brock, Bernard L. *Methods of Rhetorical Criticism: A Twentieth-Century Perspective.* New York: Harper & Row, Publishers, 1972.

Book With Three Authors

Meyer, John; Kain, John F.; and Wohl, Martin. *The Urban Transportation Problem.* Cambridge, Mass.; Harvard University Press, 1968.

Book With More Than Three Authors

Wahlke, John; Eulau, Heinz; Buchanan, William; and Ferguson, LeRoy C. *The Legislative System.* New York: John Wiley & Sons, Inc., 1962.

Book With an Association as Author
National Manpower Council. *Government and Manpower.* New York: Columbia University Press, 1964.

Pseudonym, Author's Real Name Known
Clemens, Samuel [Mark Twain]. *Huckleberry Finn.* New York: Harcourt, Brace & World, 1969.

Author's Name Not on Title Page, But Known
[Hamilton, Alexander; Madison, James; and Jay, John.] *The Federalist Papers.* Edited by Jacob Cook. Middletown, Conn: Wesleyan University Press, 1961.

Book's Author Anonymous
The Holy Quran. Washington, D.C.: Islamic Center, 1960.

Book By Editor, Compiler, or Translator: No Other Author Listed
Editors
Theobold, Robert, ed. *Social Policies for America in the Seventies: Nine Divergent Views.* New York: Doubleday & Co., Inc., 1968.

Compilers
Lindsay, Robert, and Neu, John, comps. *French Political Pamphlets, 1547-1684.* Madison: University of Wisconsin Press, 1969.

Translators
Molinaro, Ursule, trans. *Beowulf.* New York: Farrar, Straus & Giroux, Inc., 1957.

Translated or Edited Books in which the Author is Known
Stolper, Gustav; Hauser, Karl; and Borchardt, Knut. *The German Economy, 1870 to Present.* Translated by Toni Stoper. New York: Harcourt, Brace, & World, 1969.

Edited or Translated Work in which the Editor Is More Important than the Author
Riordon, William L., ed. *Plunkitt of Tammany Hall,* by George Washington Plunkitt. New York: E. P. Dutton & Co., 1900.

Books, Multivolume
Inbau, Fred E.; Thompson, James R.; and Sowle, Claude R. *Cases and Comments on Criminal Justice.* Vol. 1. Mineola, N.Y.: The Foundation Press, Inc., 1968.

Book in a Series
Gutteridge, W. F. *The Military in African Politics.* Studies in African History. London: Methuen & Co. Ltd., 1969.

Comments: If a book is part of a series the citations should include the name of the series and the volume number. Spell out the author's name in full unless he is commonly known by his initials.

Book in a Series, One Author, Several Volumes, Each With a Different Title
Mallet, Charles Edward. *The Medieval University and Colleges Founded in the Middle Ages.* Vol. 1. The History of Oxford University. New York: Barnes & Noble, Inc., 1968.

Paperback Edition of a Book, First Published in Hard Cover
Wildavsky, Aaron. *The Politics of the Budgetary Process.* Paperback. Boston: Little, Brown and Co., paperback, 1964.

Introduction to Book by Another Author
Inkeles, Alex. Introduction to *The Process of Modernization,* by John Brode. Cambridge: Harvard University Press, 1969.

Citation in One Book from Another Book
Wheeler-Bennett, John W. *The Nemesis of Power.* London: MacMillan & Co., Ltd., 1954.

Book Review
Ranger, Willard. "International Politics, Law, and Organization," review of *Regionalism and World Order,* by Ronald Yales. *The American Political Science Review* 60 (September 1966): 759.

Literature
Plays and Long Poems
Shaw, George Bernard. *The Devil's Disciple.* Baltimore, Md.: Penguin Books, Inc., 1955.

Short Poems
Poe, Edgar Allan. "To Helen." *Eternal Passion in English Poetry.* Freeport, N.Y.: Books for Libraries, Inc., 1969.

Bible
The Bible. Revised Standard Version.

Classical Works
Caesar, Julius. *The Gallic War.* Translated by H. J. Edwards. Cambridge: Harvard University Press, 1965.

Modern Edition of Classical Work
Augustine. *City of God.* Translated by Marcus Dods. New York: Modern Library, 1950.

Article, Chapter, or Other Part of a Book.
Sherfey, Mary Jane. "A Theory on Female Sexuality." *Sisterhood Is Powerful.* Edited by Robin Morgan. New York: Vintage Books, Random House, 1970.

Works Available in Microfilm
Tauber, Abraham. *Spelling Reform in the United States.* Ann Arbor, Mich.: University Microfilms, 1958.

Encyclopedias, Almanacs, and Other Reference Works
Signed Articles

International Encyclopedia of the Social Sciences, 5th ed., s.v. "Systems Analysis: Political Systems," by William C. Mitchell.

Unsigned Articles

Oxford Dictionary of National Biography, s.v. "Akers-Douglas, Aretas."

Periodical: Author Given
Consecutive Pages

Fellman, David. "Constitutional Law in 1958-1959." *American Political Science Review* 54 (1960): 168-70.

Nonconsecutive Pages

Lissner, Will. "Protection of the Author's Reprint Rights." *American Journal of Economics* 28 (April 1969): 2, 11.

Magazine Article, No Author Given

"Tax Changes for 1971: The Plans Take Shape." *U.S. News & World Reports,* 5 October 1970, p. 91.

Newspapers
American

Wilson, George C., "Copter Force Hits Camp Near Hanoi," *The Washington Post* 351 (24 November 1970) : 1A, 14A.

Foreign

Times (London) , 1 December 1970, p. 10.

    Comment: Include name of city for foreign or little known newspapers.

Proceedings of a Meeting or Conference: Reproduced

The Seventy-seventh Annual Conference of the International Chiefs of Police. "Proceedings of the Conference of the International Chiefs of Police." Atlantic City: C.I.C.P. October 6, 1970. Mimeographed.

Minutes of a Meeting: Not Reproduced
Capitol Improvement Advisory Committee. Washington, D.C. Minutes of Meeting of 5 May 1971.

Paper Read or Speech Delivered at a Meeting
Mitchell, John N. "Legalized Wiretapping." Paper read at the Seventy-seventh Annual Conference of International Chiefs of Police, October 5 , 1970, at Atlantic City, N.J. Mimeographed.

Thesis or Dissertation
Thomson, William John. "Variables Affecting Human Discrimination Processes." Ph.D. diss., Stanford University, 1969.

Legal Citations
Federal Statute
Administrative Procedure Act. @11-6 U.S.C.@1009 (1964).

State Statute
Blue Sky Law. @2 New York General Business Code @ 352, McKinney, 1962.

Court Case
Kerr v. California, 357 U.S. 50 (1963).

Law Review Articles
Ebb, *The Grundig-Consten Case Revisited.* 115 Univ. Penn. L. Rev., 1969.

Statutory Material
U.S. *Constitution,* art. 2, sec. 1.

Material from Manuscript Collections
Washington, D.C. Library of Congress. Tappan Papers. Diary of Lewis Tappan, 25 February 1835 to 29 August 1838.

Radio and Television Programs

C.B.S. "C.B.S. Evening News," 8 December 1970, "Rube Goldberg Dies," Walter Cronkite, reporter.

Interview

Rauh, Carl, Deputy Attorney General for the District of Columbia. Washington. Interview, December 2, 1970.

Mimeographed or Other Nonprinted Reports

American University. "Codebook: Baker Survey of Local Elected Officials." Mimeographed. Washington: American School of Government.

Pamphlet

Effer, Harold T. *Joseph Clark, Your Man in Washington.* Office of Sen. Clark. Washington, D.C., Fall, 1970.

Letters

Pittsburgh, Pa. Hillman Library University of Pittsburgh. Political Papers of Governor David Leo Lawrence. Lawrence to Barr, 8 November 1958.

Documents

Citing documents is always a difficult problem, for their form is totally unlike that of books and magazines. The card catalogue is a good guide and the following general rules should help. Include in this order:

1. The country (U.S. etc.)
2. Branch of government (legislative, executive, etc.)
3. The subbranch or subbranches (House, Committee on Education and Labor, etc.)

The branches of subbranches can become complicated: a careful examination of the document itself, its entry in the card catalogue, or the *Government Organization Manual* (see page 116) should give you an idea as to the sequence of organization. This information is followed by the title (underlined), the name of the series or sequence, and the facts of publication. The following examples include the most commonly cited government publications.

Congressional Documents
Bills
U.S. Congress. House. *Higher Education Act of 1965.* 89th Cong., 1st sess., H.R. 9567.

U.S. Congress. Senate. *Metropolitan Planning Act.* 88th Cong., 2nd sess., S. 885.

Debates
U.S. Congress. Senate. *Congressional Record*, 91st Congress, 2nd sess., 1970, 25, pt. 511:665.

Report
U.S. Congress. House. *Higher Education Act of 1965*, 89th Cong., 1st sess., 1965, H.R. 9567.

Hearings
U.S. Congress. House. Committee on Ways and Means. *Hearings to Exclude from the Gross Income the First $750 of Interest Received on Deposit in Thrift Institutions, H.R. 16545*, 91st Cong., 2nd sess., 1970.

Executive Documents
From an Executive Department
U.S. Department of Interior. *Final Report to the President on the Potomac Basin: "The Nation's River."* Washington D.C.: U.S. Dept. of Interior, 1968.

Presidential Papers
U.S. President. "Statement by the President on Actions and Recommendations for the Federal City, January 31, 1969." *Weekly Compilation of Presidential Documents*, 5. February 3, 1970.

International Documents
International Organizations

League of Nations. Secretariat. *Administration of Territory* (O.J.).March 1920, p. 52.

United Nations. General Assembly. 14th Session, November 20, 1959. *General Assembly Resolution 1386*, A/4353.

Treaties

U.S. *Statutes at Large,* vol. 43, pt. 2 (December 1923-March 1925). "Naval Arms Limitation Treaty," February 26, 1922.

State and Local Documents
State

New Jersey. Office of the Governor. Governor's Select Commission on Civil Disorder. *Report for Action.* Trenton: Office of the Governor, 1968.

City

New York, N.Y. Mayor's Office. Mayor's Task Force on Reorganization of New York City Government. *The Mayor's Task Force on Reorganization of New York City Government: Report and Proposed Local Law.* New York: Institute of Public Administration, 1966.

FOOTNOTES

Every speech includes some material that does not belong totally to the speaker. This material may be controversial, especially significant to the central argument, obscure and unique, or a direct quotation taken from outside sources. These constitute basic types of materials that should be footnoted in both papers and speeches. However, most speakers are not required to use the same type of form as writers because most of their footnotes will be in the text of the speech and not included separately at the bottom of a page or at the end of the work. But the audiences of speakers, like those of readers, need to know the sources of certain information in order to determine its validity and significance. This determines their overall response to the total work. Speakers wish to include information concerning the sources for several of the following reasons: they do not wish to plagiarize or steal ideas; they wish to have a well-known name or authority to lend weight to their ideas; or they wish to let the audience know where they can find the information in case they disbelieve the facts.

The reason for footnoting will determine the amount of information that the speaker includes. It may not always be necessary to include all of the information desired by regular footnote form. If a few lines from Coleridge's poem "Rime of the Ancient Mariner" are used, a speaker needs only to mention the poet and poem, not the exact lines. However, if the major argument is hung on a statistic or a fact, the speaker should include specific information on how to find this so that the audience members can check it for themselves. The text of a speech might read like the following: "According to the Minnesota Poll found in the Minneapolis *Tribune* on Sunday, July 16, 1972, page 4B, 24% of all adults in the United States believed that the Republican party stands for big business and tax breaks for the wealthy."

Rhetorical Criticism

Mass communication systems have made rhetorical discourse more influential than ever. An understanding of rhetorical criticism helps to understand and evaluate this abundance of messages. Rhetorical criticism describes what the speaker is doing, how to interpret what he is saying, and how to evaluate his ideas and their ramifications. Rhetorical criticism also may fulfill many secondary purposes. These may include anything from improving a political candidate's speaking style to completing an assignment required for a speech course. Rhetorical criticism examines the means used and attempts to gauge its effects.

The specific methods that critics use to analyze speeches are varied, as can be seen by examining the different perspectives and approaches listed in table 5. According to Robert L. Scott and Bernard L. Brock in *Methods of Rhetorical Criticism: A Twentieth-Century Perspective,* there are three major perspectives for criticism. Each of them has two basic approaches: 1. Traditional—Neo-Aristotelian and historical; 2. Experiential—eclectic and sociocultural-psychological; 3. The "New Rhetorics"—grammatical-semantical and dramatistic. The table also lists writers and works relevant to the style of these specific areas. Characteristics of the three major perspectives are given as well as a possible approach to the organization of a paper or speech on rhetorical criticism. For a total understanding of these approaches, it is recommended that the student read Scott and Brock's book, as well as some of the works noted in

Part II. All of the quoted material in the table also is taken from this book.[1]

BEGINNING CRITICISM

Beginning students of speech criticism should understand some basic points on how to listen to and evaluate a speech given by all varieties of speakers. Speeches should be first of all evaluated as living presentations, not as pieces of literature. If a speech script must be evaluated, the background and environment of the speaker, the occasion, and the audience should be studied in order to attempt a reconstruction of the original living experience. Several critical questions may be used to begin with:

1. Are the choice of subjects, its treatment, and delivery appropriate to the speaker, audience, and occasion?
2. Is the choice and handling of the material done in a knowledgeable, responsible, and honest manner?
3. Do the choice of material and the delivery of the speech keep the audience interested?
4. Is the organization clearcut and easily followed by the audience?
5. What did the speaker wish to accomplish? Did he accomplish it?

A more detailed means of evaluation is found in table 6, which is a speech instructor's critique sheet. All of the major aspects of a speech such as topic, thesis, introduction, organization, developmental techniques, conclusion, style, delivery, and originality are mentioned, as well as specific things to notice about each of them. All of these aspects must be seen in relation to their appropriateness to the speaker, occasion, and audience.

. . . .

[1]Robert L. Scott and Bernard L. Brock, *Methods of Rhetorical Criticism: A Twentieth-Century Perspective* (New York: Harper & Row, 1972), pp. 339-340.

TABLE 5 / Criticism Chart

Major Perspective	Orientation	Assumptions	Consensus	Specific Approach	A Suggested Procedure
TRADITIONAL	Concentration on speaker and his response to rhetorical problems.	"1. Society is stable; people, circumstances, rhetorical principles are fundamentally the same throughout history. 2. Rhetoricians have discovered the essential principles of public discourse. 3. Rhetorical concepts are reasonably discrete and can be studied apart from one another in the process of analyzing rhetorical discourse. 4. A reasonably close word-thought-thing-relationship exists. Rhetorical concepts accurately describe an assumed reality."	"Rhetoricians generally agree on what the ideal rhetorical process is."	Neo-Aristotelian	I. Physical setting (season, weather of the day) II. Temper of the times (including specific causes) III. Personal history of speaker IV. Politics and temper of the times as they affect the speaker and occasion. V. Immediate physical setting as it affects the audience, speaker, and vice-versa. VI. The speaker in the audience's eyes (physical image, knowledge and acceptance of) VII. Speaker's delivery VIII. Immediate audience reaction IX. Speech preparation A. Background and motivations of strategy B. Speaker's awareness of his own image C. Reactions to speech during preparatory stages and corrections made X. Response, reactions to and effects of the speech after its delivery XI. Critical evaluations of the speech A. Its effectiveness in communicating B. Criticisms of strategy used to accomplish the purpose C. Distinctive characteristics of style D. Criticisms of delivery in perspective

TABLE 5 / Continued

Major Perspective	Orientation	Assumptions	Consensus	Specific Approach	A Suggested Procedure
EXPERIENTIAL	"No single elements or rhetorical principle can be assumed as the starting point for criticism. Thus, the critic, depending on his sensitivity and knowledge, must make the fundamental choice of emphasis."	"1. Society is in a continual state of process. 2. An infinite combination of concepts, strategies, and principles are available for the study of public discourse. 3. Any system of categorizing is arbitrary and does not accurately reflect an assumed external reality for extended periods of time."	"No special pattern exists for the study of public discourse. Therefore, discourse must continually be studied afresh."	Historical	I. Historical background for speaker's ideas (his predecessors, etc.) II. Speaker's personal background III. Forces of opposition and speaker's strategy to overcome them.

				Eclectic	I. Description of incidents surrounding speech
					 II. Rhetorical context
					   A. Speaker reputation
					   B. Audience expectations
					 III. Speaker's purpose
					 IV. Speaker's strategy analyzed
					   A. Organization
					   B. Techniques
					   C. Style
					   D. Delivery
					   E. Tone
					 V. Justification of strategy

				Sociocultural-Psychological	I. Strategy
					   A. Set up basic archtypal patterns
					   B. Relate specific situations, countries, people, etc., to the general archtypal patterns.

TABLE 5 / *Continued*

Major Perspective	Orientation	Assumptions	Consensus	Specific Approach	A Suggested Procedure
					II. Motivations from the speaker's experience and personality which led him to his type of strategy. III. Characteristics of the times and of the audience which make them susceptible to the strategy.

"NEW RHETORICS"	"Rhetoric and criticism must find a starting point in the interaction of man and his social environment."	"1. Society is in process, but fairly stable relationships can be found that govern man's interactions with his environment.
		2. A flexible framework may be constructed for the study of public discourse.
		3. Man's symbol system influences his perception of reality."
			"A unified rhetorical framework is necessary for the productive study of rhetoric and criticism."	Semantical-Grammatical	I. Explanation of what this approach hopes to accomplish.
					II. General stylistic characteristics
					  A. Characteristic themes
					  B. Characteristic images
					III. Specific characteristics
					  A. Organization
					  B. Examination of words
					    1. What they reveal about
					      a. Time factor
					      b. Tone
					    2. Connotation
					    3. Imagery
					    4. Language classification
					    5. Type of emphasis
					    6. Rhythm
					IV. Placed in the larger context of culture
					  A. Language as it helps to sustain a "climate" and provides a pattern for a cultural climate.

TABLE 5 / *Continued*

Major Perspective	Orientation	Assumptions	Consensus	Specific Approach	A Suggested Procedure
				Dramatistic	Burke's "Dramatistic Pentad" The following aspects are examined in order to reveal the speaker's world view: I. Act (what was done) II. Scene (when or where it was done) III. Agent (who did it) IV. Agency (how it was done) V. Purpose (why it was done)

SPEECH INSTRUCTOR'S CRITICISM

A student of speech also needs to be aware of criticism because either an instructor or a contest judge evaluates everything that he does. This criticism should not be thought of in an unfavorable manner, because good comments as well as negative ones are made. Any negative comments are merely suggestions for improvement and should be welcomed. Table 6 is a sample of one used by the author of this reasearch guide. The numbers are useful because they gauge the instructor's general impressions without diverting too much of his attention away from the speech. Having boxes containing general evaluations of appropriateness to speaker, occasion, and audience will bring this important concept to the student's attention and will encourage him to concentrate upon it in subsequent speeches. Additional comments can be jotted down on the side after the speech is completed. If a student has a copy of the evaluation sheet used by his instructor before he begins giving speeches, he can judge more accurately the aspects upon which he should focus when preparing and delivering subsequent speeches.

GRADING SPEECHES

The following scholastic criteria for grading speeches are from Robert T. Oliver, "The Eternal (and Infernal) Problem of Grades," *The Speech Teacher,* IX (January, 1960), pp. 9-10. (Reprinted with permission of the publishers.)

> I. Normally, an average speech (C) should meet the following standards:
> A. Conform to type assigned (expository, persuasive, etc.)
> B. Conform reasonable to the time limit.
> C. Exhibit sound organization: a clear purpose adequately supported by main ideas that are easily identified.
> D. Fulfill any special requirements of the assignment—such as, to use three illustrations, or statistics, or authority, etc.

TABLE 6 / Speech Instructor's Critique Sheet

GRADING SCALE
(where specific values are not given)
1—below average (needs improvement)
2—average (ok could be improved)
3—above average (good)
4—superior (done in an excellent manner, no
    changes suggested even of a minor nature)

_____
(Name of Speaker)

_____
(Speech Type—Specific Assignment)

_____
(Date)

_____
(Name of Evaluator)

		Appropriate to					ADDITIONAL COMMENTS
		Speaker		Occasion		Audience	
		yes	no	yes	no	yes	no
I. Topic or Subject							
A. Appropriate to assignment:	1 2 3 4						
B. Scope: too broad too narrow							
good (adequate)							
III. Thesis							
A. Clarity of central idea:	1 2 3 4						
III. Introduction: in total:	1 2 3 4						
A. Attract attention:	1 2 3 4						
B. Introduce subject:	1 2 3 4						
IV. Organization							
A. Clear division of ideas:	1 2 3 4						
B. Appropriate order:	1 2 3 4						
V. Development and Techniques							
A. Idea was fully developed:	1 2 3 4						
B. Ideas were proved:	1 2 3 4						
C. Techniques were appropriate							
and interesting:	1 2 3 4						
D. Emphasis (where?):	1 2 3 4						
VI. Conclusion							
A. Wrap up thought?	1 2 3 4						
B. Leave a favorable impression?	1 2 3 4						
VII. Style							
A. Word choice: in total:	1 2 3 4						
1. Clarity:	1 2 3 4						
2. Brevity:	1 2 3 4						
3. Variety:	1 2 3 4						
B. Use of imagery:	1 2 3 4						

TABLE 6 / *continued*

		Appropriate to					ADDITIONAL COMMENTS
		Speaker		Occasion		Audience	
		yes	no	yes	no	yes	no
C. Variation in sentences: 1 2 3 4							
D. Use of misc. stylistic techniques: 1 2 3 4							
VIII. Delivery, in total: 1 2 3 4							
A. Vocal aspect:							
1. Appropriate volume: 1 2 3 4							
2. Articulation and enuncia- tion: 1 2 3 4							
3. Pronunciation: 1 2 3 4							
4. Projection: 1 2 3 4							
5. Vocal variations:							
a. Rate—too fast too slow ok							
b. Use of pauses—good poor							
c. Rhythm patterns—too many ok							
d. Pitch—too high too low ok							
e. Volume—varied poorly good							
f. Vocal quality 1 2 3 4							
6. Unnecessary noise 1 2 3 4							
B. Physical aspect							
1. Facial gesture							
a. Eye Contact: 1 2 3 4							
b. Animation: 1 2 3 4							
c. Appropriate to mood and context: 1 2 3 4							
2. Bodily gestures							
a. Good posture: 1 2 3 4							
b. Random movement: 1 2 3 4							
c. Appropriate, motivated and relaxed gestures: 1 2 3 4							
d. Use of notes: 1 2 3 4							
3. Adapt to audience: 1 2 3 4							

IX. Originality: Idea seemed original—not original
    Approach was original—not original

> E. Be intellectually sound in developing a topic of worth with adequate and dependable evidence.
> F. Exhibit reasonable directness and communicativeness in delivery.
> G. Be correct grammatically and in pronounciation and articulation.
> H. Be ready for presentation on date assigned.

II. The better than average (B) speech should meet the foregoing tests and also:

> A. Contain elements of vividness and special interest in its style.
> B. Be of more than average stimulative quality in challenging the audience to think or in arousing depth of response.
> C. Demonstrate skill in winning understanding of unusually difficult concepts of process: or in winning agreement from auditors initially inclined to disagree with the speaker's purpose.
> D. Establish rapport of a high order through style and delivery which achieve a genuinely communicative circular response.

III. The superior speech (A) not only meets the foregoing standards but also:

> A. Constitutes a genuinely individual contribution by the speaker to the thinking of the audience.
> B. Achieves a variety and flexibility of mood and manner suited to the multiple differentiation of thinking and feeling demanded by the subject matter and by the speaker-audience relations.
> C. Achieves a demonstrable progression from the initial uncertainty (of knowledge or belief) held by the audience toward the subject, by orderly process, toward a final resolution of the uncertainty in a conclusion that evolves naturally from the material used by the speaker.
> D. Illustrates skillful mastery of internal transitions and of emphasis in presentation of the speaker's ideas.

IV. Speakers must be classified below average (D or F) if they are deficient in some or several of the factors required for the "C" speech.

Part II

ANNOTATED LISTING OF BASIC REFERENCES

Annotated Listing of Basic References

INTRODUCTION

The following section consists of an annotated list of reference works that were selected for their usefulness to students of speech. Not all the major reference works in a field of study are given, and not all fields of study are included. If a student is majoring or minoring in speech, or even taking an introductory speech course, it is assumed that neither he nor his audience is well-versed in another subject area. Therefore, the reference works included are ones to be used by amateurs for an audience of laymen.

A list of general reference works is followed by a section on specialized fields. Emphasis is on the social sciences, particularly political science, because most speeches, discussions, and debates are centered in these areas. Finally, speech, as the target field for this research guide, has a section to itself, following the other subject areas. It includes major reference works in the area, as well as journals and bibliography of recent textbooks in the various subfields.

GENERAL REFERENCE WORKS

Almanacs

Comparative International Almanac. Morris L. Ernst and Judith A. Posner, eds. New York: Macmillan, 1967—.

Excellent source of comparative (as opposed to raw) data about nations. It contains information in the form of statistical comparisons on a variety of items such as suicide rates, phones per 1,000 population, life expectancies, literary rates, and so on. Organization is on a country-by-country basis with a topical country-by-country ranking.

The Official Associated Press Almanac. Laurence Urdang, ed. New York: Almanac Publishing Company, Inc., 1973.

The successor to the *New York Times Encyclopedic Almanac*, calls itself "the almanac with the authority of the world's largest news organization." Claims to have "More information than any other almanac available." Includes 16 full color pages of maps; summaries of 147 countries and 94 territories and dependencies; up-to-date vital statistics; records and statistics of major sports events; and 800 brief biographies of major figures living and dead.

World Almanac and Book of Facts. New York: Newspaper Enterprise Association, 1868–.

Published yearly, the *World Almanac* supplies a wealth of information in every area likely to be investigated by undergraduate students. A random sample of the broad spectrum of the work includes the latest sports records; Nobel Prize recipients; listings of colleges and universities; heads of states; brief descriptions of foreign countries; a list of United States art galleries; biographies of presidents and their wives, cabinet members, Supreme Court judges, and ambassadors; and an explanation of how to make out a will properly.

Bibliographies

Books in Print. New York: R. R. Bowker, 1947–.

Two-volume author-title series index to *The Publishers' Trade List Annual* (same publisher), it lists over 300,000 titles available from 2,250 publishers in the United States. Vol. I, the author series, lists author, co-author, editor, translator, price, imprint, publisher, year of publication, edition, number of volumes, type of binding, and if illustrated. Vol. II, the title series, lists title, author, price, publisher, editions, number of volumes, editor, and type of binding.

Book Review Digest. New York: H. W. Wilson, 1905—.

Monthly indexed reference to selected book reviews drawn from about seventy-five English and American periodicals. It is arranged by title, and has title and subject indexes. Each issue covers from 300 to 400 titles. Excerpts from several reviews and a bibliography are presented for each book.

Book Review Index. Detroit: Gale Research, 1965—.

To a great extent, this monthly review with quarterly cumulations supplements the *Book Review Digest.* The index lists current book reviews in the social and natural sciences, although no excerpts of reviews are given, and there is only an author index.

Cumulative Book Index. New York: H. W. Wilson, 1898—.

This monthly index with compilations provides a comprehensive list of books published in various areas of interest, some of which might not be found in a college library. It supplies a tabulation of publications as they come off the press and usually lists other works of each author. Included in the index and of value to the researcher, is a selected list of important government documents. Since 1925 the *Cumulative Book Index* has included books in the English language that are published outside the United States.

Directory of Information Resources in the United States. The National Referral Center for Science and Technology of the Library of Congress, Washington, D.C.: Government Printing Office. Published irregularly.

To obtain material from this source it is necessary to know precisely what information you want. This directory contains what librarians term "fugitive material," in that it is material available to the public on request only, and when the supply is exhausted it is unobtainable. This guide supplies a strong list of most federal and federally sponsored agencies (such as the East-West Center of the University of Hawaii), and describes their activities and the type of data available from each. Most of the material is in the form of printed government documents and in typewritten and mimeographed reports. The directory is published irregularly. To date only five volumes have been published.

Dissertation Abstracts. Ann Arbor: University of Michigan. University Microfilm.

As the major source of doctoral dissertations in the United States, these abstracts offer a brief abstract of each paper, the emphasis lying in the methods and conclusions of the study. A useful source for speech ideas, it is available in both microfilm and full-size editions. It is compiled monthly.

Essay and General Literature Index. New York: H. W. Wilson, 1934. (Latest supplement, 1970, by Estelle A. Fidell and Norma Freedman.)

Published semiannually with accumulations, specifically catalogs books rather than periodicals, which is helpful because essays and articles often appear in books of collected works without there being a specific reference to them in the title. This index could help locate, for example, an article on "Woodrow Wilson and Southern Congressmen" which appeared in a book (edited by Sidney Fine) titled *Recent America* (New York: Crowell-Collier and Macmillan, Inc., 1962).

Guide to Reference Books. 8th ed. Constance M. Winchell, ed. Chicago: American Library Association, 1967. Yearly supplements.

Most comprehensive of all guides of this type, the latest edition divides 7,500 titles into five categories: general reference works; humanities; social sciences; history and area studies; and the pure and applied sciences. If you do not find the appropriate reference work listed in the reference section of this book, the *Guide to Reference Books* should lead you to it.

Poole's Index to Periodical Literature, rev. ed. Boston: Houghton Mifflin, 1891.

Although not as comprehensive as the *Reader's Guide to Periodical Literature,* this is still the best index of nineteenth-century periodicals (covering approximately the years 1800-1906). It includes poems and stories and can be used to research such subjects as the cultural or political attitudes expressed in American periodicals of that time.

Readers' Guide to Periodical Literature. New York: H. W. Wilson, 1901—.

The major periodical reference book, it lists author and subject in separate indexes referring to the most popular, non-technical periodicals in the English language.

Reference Books in the Social Sciences and Humanities. Rolland E. Stevens. Champaign, Illinois: Illinois Union Bookstore, 1968—.

An annotated list of reference materials on such topics as political science, law, and public administration.

Selected United States Government Publications. Washington, D.C.: Government Printing Office, 1928—.

The government prints and mails out a biweekly list of the thousands of pamphlets, books, and periodicals published by the Government Printing Office. Writer-researchers are sent into the field by the government to initiate exhaustive research into topics as varied as black-white differences in geographic mobility, health information (menopause, varicose veins, high blood pressure, and so on), the Great Seal of the United States, heart disease in adults, United States from 1960 to 1971, boating regulations in the national park system, employment and earnings statistics for states and areas, and case studies of displaced workers. One may place one's name on the free mailing list by sending name and address to: Superintendent of Documents, United States Government Printing Office, Washington, D.C. The order form is attached to the lists. Prices vary, but most pamphlets and books cost less than comparable volumes privately printed.

Social Sciences and Humanities Index. New York: H. W. Wilson,
1916—.

Compiled quarterly this index provides the best source for
developing an academic or theoretical focus for a speech. It
indexes periodicals in the fields of drama, social science, history, religion, literature, art, etc. In June, 1965, the title of this
reference was changed from *International Index* in order to
indicate the scope of its coverage more accurately.

Vertical File Index. New York: H. W. Wilson, 1955—.

A subject and title index to selected pamphlets on many
different fields. It lists many free and/or inexpensive materials
and propaganda for current reference. Material indexed here is
not indexed anywhere else. Published monthly, except August,
with annual cumulations.

Biographies

Biography Index. New York: H. W. Wilson, 1947—.

Published quarterly with cumulations, it is the key index
to biographical material. It includes all of the biographical
references found in other indexes plus selected foreign references. Entries are arranged alphabetically with a subject index
in the back of each issue. This subject index is especially helpful
in attempting to identify important individuals in a particular
field who are receiving public attention.

Current Biography. New York: H. W. Wilson, 1940—.

Supplies unbiased sketches of contemporary personalities
in about forty different professional fields. Contains a photograph of each subject, gives the proper pronunciation of more
difficult names, and lists references for additional material.
Each issue contains an accrued list index of previous issues.
Besides the annual compilation, there are ten-year indexes.

International Who's Who. London: G. Allen, 1935—.

Published annually since 1935, this reference contains
from 8,000 to 13,000 short biographical sketches of prominent
figures of the world. Before 1935 it formed a part of the

looseleaf service called "Europa." The *International Who's Who* provides brief but reliable information on the subjects, giving name, title, dates, nationality, education, profession, career, works, and address.

Who's Who in America: A Biographical Dictionary of Notable Living Men and Women. Chicago: A. N. Marquis, 1899—.

This book has been described as "An authoritative dictionary of contemporary biography, including the best known men and women in all lines of useful and reputable achievement— names much in the public eye, not names locally but generally." The biographies fall into two groups: those selected because of their special prominence or distinction in certain fields, and those included arbitrarily due to their official position or public standing. Included are not only American citizens, but all persons of any nationality likely to be of interest to Americans. It is supplemented by: *Who Was Who in America,* for all persons deleted due to death; *The Monthly Supplement,* December 1939 to 1956; the *Supplement to Who's Who,* issued quarterly since 1957; the *Ten-Year Cumulative Index,* 1939-1949; and the *Cumulative Index* for 1951-1955. The publication major is revised and reissued biennially with monthly supplements.

Current Events

The Annual Register of World Events. New York: St. Martin's Press, 1758—.

A British publication emphasizing Great Britain and the Commonwealth. It is considered one of the best summaries of year-by-year events. It covers political as well as nonpolitical areas such as economics, the fine arts, and speeches are outlined. The Register is written in notable prose and the entries are integrated into quarterly reports.

Facts on File: World News Digest. New York: Facts on File, 1940—.

Records the events of each week in an unbiased and concise style. Each news item is filed and reported under a specific heading such as world affairs, national affairs, sports, finance, and the like. Each publication also includes a reference to any previous article on the same topic. However, sources are not listed. Four five-year indexes have been issued so far for the years 1946-1950, 1951-1955, 1956-1961, and 1962-1967.

Newspaper Index. Chicago Tribune, Los Angeles Times, The New Orleans Times-Picayune, The Washington Post. Wooster, Ohio: The Micropublishers, 1972—.

Published monthly since January, 1972, the Index is compiled from the microfilmed edition of each of the four newspapers, which represent generally the four sections of the United States. It is intended as a key to the newspapers, and the reader is always referred back to the newspaper itself for complete details in context. National, international, regional, state and local news are indexed, and a descriptive statement attempts to reflect the emphasis given to the news items by the newspapers. The Index also includes letters to the editor, editorials, syndicated columns, and all reviews. Classified death notices are not indexed. The Index is divided in two files—subject and name. The name index is an alphabetical listing by last name of people in the news; the subject file is a keyword index, e.g., The American Civil Liberties Union is under the subject heading Civil Liberties Union, American.

New York Times Index. New York: The New York Times, 1913—.

The major reference source for an accurate chronological list of important events. Published semimonthly with annual cumulations since 1930, this publication presents an extensive and detailed look at the world news as reported by the *New York Times.* It cites the date, page, and column with many cross references, and serves as a reference for material in other newspapers as well. One of the features students find most attractive is the brief synopsis under each entry, which frequently makes reference to the newspaper itself unnecessary. An earlier index covering the years 1851-1858 and 1860-1905 is available on microfilm.

Encyclopedias

Most people instinctively turn to a general reference encyclopedia as their first source of reference, and they are well advised to do so. A good encyclopedia contains not only a great deal of important substantive information, but also useful bibliographies, cross references, and other guides to help in conducting further research. Encyclopedias, however, vary in at least three important ways:

1. *Quality.* Many encyclopedias are authoritative and scholarly, but some are neither. Only those encyclopedias generally accepted as reliable by teachers, librarians, and scholars are listed here.
2. *Depth.* Some encyclopedias are designed for grade school and high school use, some for popular adult use, and others for scholarly use at the college level. Included here are only those suitable for research at the college level, excluding many excellent works such as the *World Book,* which is designed for elementary, high school, and general adult use.
3. *Scope.* While the term "encyclopedia" denotes an all-inclusive approach, even encyclopedias specialize. Under the proper title the strong points of each set are indicated.

Encyclopedias are especially useful in obtaining general background material, and they may be browsed through when the speaker is trying to get an idea for a speech topic. Under no circumstances should the entire speech be based on information taken only from encyclopedias.

Collier's Encyclopedia. New York: Crowell-Collier and Macmillan, 1969.

Strong, clearly written, well-indexed general encyclopaedia. It is reliable and often has enough depth for freshman and sophomore assignments, although it is not exhaustive. It is a good first source with good bibliographies.

The Encyclopedia Americana. New York: The Americana Corporation, 1972.

The strongest source for all aspects of American life and culture. Articles are written by leading scholars, with especially strong coverage of recent American history. The bibliography is extensive and so authoritative that it is frequently consulted by librarians.

Encyclopedia of Associations. Detroit: Gale Research, 1970.

Listing of nearly 13,000 varied organizations or reference centers where the speaker may send for data, industry surveys, specialized publications, background material, and hard-to-find information. The encyclopedia also gives details concerning the organization itself—such as its activities and purposes, its headquarters, its publications, and its research and educational programs. Indexed by titles and key words.

Encyclopaedia Britannica. Chicago: Encyclopaedia Britannica, 1971.

Although no longer British-oriented, this is without question the single most extensive and detailed general encyclopedia. Some articles in the traditional fields of the humanities, arts, and sciences have become classics. In scope and depth the major articles are equivalent to specialized books on the subject, but unlike ordinary books a *Britannica* article is assuredly written by an outstanding authority in his field. The assistance of cross references and "sign post" articles to lead to related material in other fields is also given.

Encyclopedia International. New York: Grolier, 1969.

It is difficult to publish a new encyclopedia that can compete in scope and quality with the established sets, but the *Encyclopedia International* is doing just that. This is a readable general encyclopedia with unusual headings and subheadings that heighten reader interest. It also includes such helpful and practical information as lists of colleges, study aids, and career guides.

Lincoln Library of Essential Information. Buffalo, New York: Frontier Press, 1963.

Includes information for the average reader in the following subject areas, which are further divided into subheads: English language, literature, history, geography and travel, science, mathematics, economic and useful arts, education, biography, and miscellany. It contains maps, illustrations, and a comprehensive index. It is revised with every printing.

Opinion Polls

California Poll. San Francisco: Survey Research Services.

The California electorate is one of the most significant in the nation as a harbinger of future trends. This poll is concentrated within the State of California. It polls Californians on the hottest issue at the time and publishes results between thirty-five to forty-five times a year.

Gallup Opinion Index. Princeton, N.J.: Gallup International, 1965–.

Although most Americans are familiar with the Gallup opinion polls published regularly in many newspapers, these polls are often neglected by undergraduate researchers because of the difficulty of locating a particular poll in an unindexed newspaper. This monthly publication offers an answer to this problem through the publication of thirteen to fifteen monthly surveys covering a wide range of subjects, from Vietnam to "Most Admired Woman."

Roper Public Opinion Poll. Williamstown, Mass.: Williams College.

The most exhaustive file of poll data in existence, this source concentrates on all academic and professional poll and survey groups from around the world. The surveys and studies are available to students on cards or tapes at quite reasonable rates.

SPECIALIZED REFERENCE WORKS

Art, Pure and Applied

Art Index. New York: H. W. Wilson, 1929—.

Indexes periodicals and museum bulletins according to author and subject in the fields of ceramics, engraving, graphic arts, architecture, decoration and ornament, archaeology, photography, etc., and includes exhibitions and reproductions of individual artists. It is published quarterly with annual cumulations.

Costume Index. Isabel Monro and E. E. Cook. New York: H. W. Wilson, 1937; suppl., 1957.

Indexes costume plates found in several hundred books, of all periods of history and all nationalties. Alphabetically arranged by subject, except for 19th and 20th centuries, which are arranged first by century, then by subject. There are no illustrations of stage or Biblical costumes, and such items as medals or insignia are shown only as part of the costume, not in detail separately.

Encyclopedia of Furniture. Joseph Aronson. New York, Crown, 1965.

Provides dependable initial information concerning furniture styles, periods, inspiration of designs, the nature of their materials, etc. It is arranged according to topics and contains many illustrations and a bibliography arranged alphabetically by country or period.

Encyclopedia of Painting. Bernard S. Myers, ed. New York: Crown, 1955.

Alphabetically arranged encyclopedia (except for Oriental painters who are grouped by period under country headings) which gives an overview of outstanding painters, movements, styles, and techniques from all periods of history and from all countries. It includes biographies; many illustrations, partly colored; and cross references.

Encyclopedia of World Art. New York: McGraw-Hill, 1959-68.

Fifteen-volumes, edited by international scholars, it is both critical and documentary. Each volume is divided into two sections, the first relating history of certain art works; the second contains illustrations of works treated in Section One.

Business and Economics

Business Education Index. New York: Delta Pi Epsilon Fraternity, 1940—.

For any student wishing to give a speech concerning business education, this source (published annually) indexes business education articles according to author and subject.

Business Periodicals Index. New York: H. W. Wilson, 1958—.

A subject-index to periodicals in the various fields of business such as insurance, labor management, management, marketing, taxation, accounting, business and finance, and advertising. Formerly a part of *Industrial Arts Index,* it is published monthly, except for July, and has annual cumulations.

Economic Almanac. New York: New York National Industrial Conference Board, 1940—.

Although not a comprehensive work, this almanac contains information about business, labor, and government in the more prominent political powers of the world. The statistics of the United States are the most complete. It also contains a general index, a special index on Canada, and a glossary of terms. One can learn, for example, how much the average production worker in Los Angeles earns per hour, or how many people will be employed in certain occupations by 1975.

Index of Economic Journals. American Economic Association. Homewood, Ill., Irwin, 1961-67.

Consisting of seven volumes published between 1961 and 1967, the set indexes economic journals dating from 1886-1965. It is one of the better guides for students interested in giving a more comprehensive speech on a subject in the area of economics.

McGraw-Hill Dictionary of Modern Economics. Douglas Greenwald, ed. New York: McGraw-Hill, 1965.

This excellent handbook of economic and business terms and organizations was written for the nonspecialist and is supplemented by charts, tables and diagrams.

Moody's Industrial Manual: American and Foreign. W. Lloyd Warner. New York: Moody's Investors Service, 1954—.

Appearing annually, it is a comprehensive source of industrial corporation information. Includes history, background, subsidiaries, business and products, important plants and properties, mergers, and acquisitions. Such details as the names of officers and directors, dates of annual meetings, and the number of employees and stockholders are also included. The most important companies are followed by a capital structure table that gives information concerning stock and bond issues. It supersedes *Moody's Manual of Investment,* 1909—.

Sources of Business Information. Rev. Ed. Edwin T. Coman, Jr. Los Angeles: Univ. of California Press, 1964.

Contains bibliographies and material which will assist in gaining information on firms, individuals, facts, real estate, insurance, marketing, accounting, management, automation, statistics, finance, and industrial relations, just to name a few. It is limited to American and Canadian publications, with only a few from England.

Standard and Poor's. New York: Standard and Poor's, 1926—.

Always kept up-to-date with revised editions, it contains information about corporations and is published periodically in two sections: the first section contains descriptions of companies and news items on white paper; the second section, printed on yellow paper, is an index and guide that shows page numbers of the company descriptions and contains a topical index to the news items. Information given includes company earnings, debts, affiliations, dividends given, names of officials, etc.

United Nations World Economic Survey. New York: United Nations Statistical Office, 1945–.

Yearly charts interpret the economy trends of the world in this survey. This book spawns a supplement of detailed studies of entire continental regions.

Wall Street Journal Index. New York: Dow Jones, 1889–.

Appearing monthly, it indexes material that has appeared in the daily *Wall Street Journal.* It is divided into two parts: corporation news and general news.

Education

The Annual Guide to Graduate Study. Karen C. Hegener. Princeton, N.J.: Peterson's Guides.

Such basic facts as the size of library facilities, financial aid, faculty research, and student life are outlined field by field, area by area.

Dictionary of Education. 2nd ed. Carter V. Good, ed. New York: McGraw-Hill, 1959.

Comprehensive source of professional terms and concepts in education that includes keys to pronunciations and abbreviations. Excluded are names of publications, places, organizations and institutions, school systems, people, etc., except where a movement, plan, or method is represented by the name.

Education Index. New York: H. W. Wilson, 1932–.

This reference, published monthly, except July and August, with compilations, is a subject index to educational periodicals, yearbooks, and bulletins, and the publications of the United States Office of Education from the year 1929. It indexes the answers to such questions as: What is the latest method of educating the mentally handicapped? How much money is being spent by the Federal government on education?

Encyclopedia of Educational Research. 3rd ed. Chester W. Harris, ed. New York: Macmillan, 1960.

The subject areas are listed alphabetically and are given a brief summary. A list of articles precedes the subject treatment and the index is found in the middle of the volume. A critical evaluation, synthesis, and interpretation of all pertinent research in education is found for each topic. There is also some information on closely related fields.

How to Locate Educational Information and Data. Carter Alexander and Arbid Burke, Jr. New York: Teachers College Press, 1958.

Although it is directed toward the education major, other students may benefit from this handbook's basic instruction in the use of the library. It describes reference sources, card catalogs, periodical indexes, bibliographies, and government documents, enabling the student to locate the information that he requires.

Random House Guide to Graduate Study in the Arts and Sciences. E. R. Wasserman and E. E. Switzer. New York: Random House, 1967.

This guide summarizes graduate programs in all fields and contains helpful chapters on the nature of graduate study, how to apply to a graduate school, and test questions from the Graduate Record Examination.

Undergraduate Study Abroad. Stephen A. Freeman. New York: Institute of International Education, 1966.

Comprehensive guide that presents all the important dates concerning overseas programs offered by a number of universities. The programs range from summer to full-year schedules, some of which require a foreign language, others that do not.

United Nations World Survey of Education. Paris: UNESCO, 1955–.

It has been published four times, but has not, to date, followed a formal publishing schedule. The four volumes extant deal with educational organizations and statistics (1955); primary education (1958); secondary education (1961); and higher education (1966).

Language

The American Thesaurus of Slang. 2nd ed. Compiled by Lester Berrey and Milvin Van Den Bark. New York: Crowell, 1953.

Traces the history of mainly American expressions. The terms are grouped by subject and the index lists in alphabetical order both the slang term and the conventional English term. An appendix titled "Slang Origins" traces the history of most of the entries.

Bibliography of Vocabulary Studies. Edgar Dale and Donald Reichert. Columbus, Ohio: Bureau of Educational Research, Ohio State University, 1957.

It is important that an effective speaker have good command of the language. In order to have this, he must have an extensive vocabulary. This source will lead him to studies that will help him in his endeavor.

Burton's Cyclopedia of Wit and Humor. William E. Burton. 1872. Repr. New York: Garrett, 1969.

Edited by the playwright, actor, and founder of *Burton's Gentleman's Magazine,* this is a worldwide anthology of humor, including examples of American, British, Irish, and Scotch comic writing. It is an invaluable source of attention-getting material for any speaker, and especially those involved in after-dinner speaking or entertaining speaking in general.

Dictionary of Slang and Unconventional English. Eric Partridge. New York: Macmillan, 1967.

Alphabetical arrangement of colloquialism, catch phrases, nicknames and vulgarisms of the English language with the definitions given in chronological order. It also includes some foreign slang terms and vulgarisms. Contemporary trends in language usage make this a useful and legitimate source with which to become acquainted.

A Dictionary of Usage and Style. Roy H. Copperud. New York: Hawthorn, 1964.

Style guide that is more a collection of what is being accepted rather than what ought to be.

The Elements of Style. William Strunk, Jr. and E. B. White. New York: Macmillan, 1959.

Originally published in 1919 by Professor Strunk of Cornell University, it was updated, expanded, and lifted to near immortality by E. B. White, that flawless stylist who has been associated with *The New Yorker* for so many years. White's chapter on what style is cannot be matched. It should be read by anyone who takes his writing or speaking seriously.

Familiar Quotations. John Bartlett, ed. Boston: Little, Brown, 1968.

Useful collection of thousands of quotations that have become part of the English language. Bartlett lists each quotation under its author and reprints it within the context of the poem, passage, or article in which it originally appeared. The authors and their quotations are listed chronologically. There is an index of authors and key words. For instance, the source of the line, "What this country needs is a good five-cent cigar," can be traced through the word "cigar" in the word index. (The source of this quotation, incidentally, is Thomas R. Marshall, the vice-president under Woodrow Wilson.)

The International Dictionary of Thoughts: An Encyclopedia of Quotations from Every Age for Every Occasion. John P. Bradley. Chicago: Ferguson, 1969.

Although its indexing is weak, this can be a valuable source of ideas and quotations for speeches. It contains around 20,000 quotations arranged by subject categories.

Magill's Quotations in Context, Second Series. Frank N. Magill. New York: Harper & Row, 1969.

Along with the quotations from the classics of poetry, drama, fiction and non-fiction, information about the context is given for each entry; a full explanation of who said what, when, where and why is also added. Both the quotations and the background information are more detailed in the Second Edition than in the first and much longer than in other quotation books. Three indexes help the speaker find the quotation he is looking for; an author index at the back, and a "first significant word" index and a key word index in the front.

The New Roget's Thesaurus of the English Language in Dictionary Form. Norman Lewis, ed. New York: Putnam, 1964.

Groups words of similar meanings together and arranges the key words and phrases in alphabetical order. A useful place to find synonyms.

Random House Dictionary of the English Language, Unabridged Edition. New York: Random House, 1966.

Although it covers only about 260,000 words (Webster's Third covers nearly a half million) this comparative newcomer to the field is already established as one of the most popular. A portion of its popularity is due to two supplement sections: a complete world atlas in color and four quite concise bilingual language dictionaries—French, German, Italian and Spanish. Unlike Webster, this dictionary's first definition after the word is the most frequently encountered.

Universal Pronouncing Dictionary of Biography and Mythology. Joseph Thomas, ed. Philadelphia: Lippincott, 1930.

Usually cited as *Lippincott's Biographical Dictionary*, it deals with biographies of significant people in history and with important subjects of mythology. It differs from other works in that it concentrates on pronunciation, which makes it especially valuable to people in the area of speech. It also contains a vocabulary of proper names and meanings.

Webster's New Dictionary of Synonyms. Springfield, Mass.: Merriam, 1968.

Brings words with similar meanings together along with some antonyms, or contrasting words. It also identifies the part of speech and the meanings. There are no pronunciation guides or etymologies.

Webster's Third New International Dictionary of the English Language, Unabridged. Springfield, Mass.: Merriam, 1961—.

Although some scholars feel that Webster's Second is superior, the *Third International* is generally accepted as perhaps *the* best of the major American single-volume unabridged dictionaries. It defines nearly half a million words, using each in a quotation that generally makes the shaded meaning instantly clear. It includes about 100,000 new words that were not in use at the time the second edition was published (1934), and is widely applauded for its coverage of the scientific and technological vocabulary.

The new edition follows the spelling of each entry with syllable separation, pronunciation, grammatical designation, plural ending of nouns, main forms of irregular verbs, capitalization, etymologies, definition, illustrative quotation, cross references, idioms usually formed with the word, the various forms the word lends itself to, and synonyms. When using Webster's Third, it is important to remember that the first definition after the word is the oldest, and the last definition is the most recent.

Law

Black's Law Dictionary. Rev. 4th ed. Henry Campbell Black. St. Paul, Minn.: West Publishing, 1968.

Defines terms and phrases of American and English jurisprudence. First published 75 years ago, Black lists, besides definitions, the useful Table of British Regnal Years, noting the sovereigns of England for more than 900 years, date of accession to the throne, and length of reign. The 1968 version includes three new features: Canons of professional ethics, canons of judicial ethics, and an outline of minimum requirements for admission to legal practice in the United States.

The Constitution of the United States of America—Analysis and Interpretation. The Legislative Reference Service of the Library of Congress of the United States. Washington, D.C.: Government Printing Office, 1964—.

Definitive work on the United States Constitution. Article by article, amendment by amendment, this authoritative work summarizes the leading cases that have shaped the interpretation of the Constitution. For example, if one wishes to know exactly what is meant by the "right to a speedy and public trial," he can find in this book a concise summary of applicable cases. The sole drawback of this book is its date of publication, since important decisions after 1964 are not included.

Index to Legal Periodicals. New York: H. W. Wilson, 1909—.

Law journals interpret the law; they also are an excellent source of public policy articles on such topics as the regulation of business. This, the best of law journal-indexes, covers roughly 300 journals and is published monthly with annual cumulations.

United States Reports. Washington, D.C.: Government Printing Office, 1790—.

Compilation of each decision rendered by the United States Supreme Court. Most decisions include majority, dissenting, and concurring opinions. These opinions contain the sweep of facts, attitudes, and legal concepts relating to the important issues that come before the Supreme Court.

Literature

Abstracts of English Studies. Chicago: University of Illinois, 1958—.

Critical and scholarly articles concerning English-American language and literature are summarized in this concise look at periodicals—both native and foreign. Published ten times a year, it provides a precise, easy index to a large mass of high-quality material.

Cambridge History of American Literature. 4 vols. William P. Trent et al., eds. Cambridge: Cambridge Univ. Press, 1917-1924.

Cambridge History of English Literature. A. W. Ward and A. R. Waller, eds. Cambridge: University Press, 1907-27 (reprinted without bibliographies, 1932).

The Concise Cambridge History of English Literature. R. C. Churchill, ed. Cambridge: University Press, 1969.

These authoritative histories deal with the influence of writers, social and political thought and movements and controversies on the literature of the respective countries.

CONCORDANCES

They are alphabetical lists of important words that have been used by certain literary figures. Each concordance deals with a single author. It will list the important words in alphabetical order and then give all of the author's works and the pages where the particular word is located. This source could help the speaker in many ways—one being to help him locate a quotation or a certain author's ideas on such concepts as "love," "religion," "acting," "horses," or "socialism." Concordances to the Bible are also useful.

Contemporary Authors. James Ethridge, ed. Detroit: Gale Research Co., 1962—.

Arranged alphabetically, it began as a quarterly and is now a semi-annual biographical reference series devoted to current authors—both well and little known—who are published by recognized presses. Familiar authors are included at the publication of their latest book.

Library of Literary Criticism: Modern British Literature. Ruth Z. Temple and M. Tucker, eds. New York: Ungar, 1966.

Three volume set containing brief excerpts of critical essays covering over 400 twentieth-century British authors, who are listed in chronological order with bibliographies of the authors' works. A quick overview of a fairly broad range of British writers.

Literary History of the United States. 2 vols. Robert E. Spiller, et al., ed. New York: Macmillan, 1963.

Over 200 American authors are included in the second volume, which has a 1,000-page bibliography listing original and secondary works—with essays on the authors. The first volume presents an authoritative view of American literature since the colonial days through the use of critical, modern essays. It contains a great listing of themes (as broad as "The American Dream") covering, among other viewpoints, philosophical and sociological stances.

Masterpieces of World Literature in Digest Form. Frank Northen Magill. New York: Harper, 1952-60.

Plays, poems, miscellaneous works as well as novels from all over the world are summarized in this manual. The resumés are arranged alphabetically, but there are also author and title indexes. Magill is well-known as the author of the *Masterplot* series, which also summarizes plots, but includes quotations and attempts to recreate the original author's style.

MLA International Bibliography. New York: Modern Language Association of America, 1922—.

Covering the period 1921 to the present, the title varies, being called *American Bibliography* from 1921 to 1955, *Annual Bibliography* from 1956 to 1962, and *MLA* (or *PMLA*) *International Bibliography* from 1963 to the present. Although largely an English language and literature critical bibliography, this annual listing of scholarship also contains an excellent, comprehensive coverage of European literature and language. Books, dissertations, and periodical articles from the previous year are categorized mainly under nationality and time period (e.g. France, Seventeenth Century).

Oxford Companion to American Literature. J. D. Hart. New York: Oxford University Press, 1965.

Oxford Companion to Classical Literature. Sir Paul Harvey. New York: Oxford University Press, 1946.

Oxford Companion to English Literature. 4th ed. Sir Paul Harvey. New York: Oxford University Press, 1946. Revised by Dorothy Eagle. Oxford: Clarendon Press, 1967.

Oxford Companion to French Literature. Sir Paul Harvey and J. E. Heseltine. Oxford: Clarendon Press, 1959.

> The *Oxford Companion* series consists of some of the most important sources in the area of literature. The entries in the books are in alphabetical order and they contain short biographies and bibliographies for authors; information concerning the style, subject matter and themes of the authors; summaries and descriptions of important plays, stories, poems, novels, essays, literary schools, movements, awards, societies, printers, etc.

The Reader's Encyclopedia. William R. Benet, ed. New York: Crowell, 1965.

> Encyclopedia and dictionary of authors, philosophers, literary terms, books, history, myths, allusions, and dates—this book is a small combination of *Bartlett's Quotations,* the *Bible,* an encyclopedia and a card catalogue.

Short Story Index. Estell Fidell. New York: H. W. Wilson, 1964-68.

> This index will help a reader locate a story if he knows the author or the title—or even if he desires to find a story dealing with a certain subject. It includes story collections, but excludes stories for children under twelve, folklore, and humorous sketches without a plot. Also includes a directory of publishers.

Subject Index to Poetry. Herbert Bruncken. Chicago: American Library Assoc., 1940.

> Arranged alphabetically by subject, this source helps the reader find a poem on a particular subject, or helps him find a poem if he does not know the title or author, but knows a line or a fragment of a line. It may help a speaker find a suitable quotation to use in a speech.

Music

Baker's Biographical Dictionary of Musicians. Rev. ed. Nicholas Slonimsky, ed. New York: Shirmer, 1958, with 1965 supplement.

Lists both contemporary and historic musicians, and their compositions. Gives biographical sketches of anyone who has made a significant contribution to music. Includes pronunciation guides, but no index. It is arranged alphabetically.

Encyclopedia of the Opera. Davis Ewen. New York: Hill & Wang, 1963.

Alphabetically arranged, comprehensive research guide giving the stories of operas, history of opera, biographies, excerpts, character discussions, a pronouncing guide at the end, and articles concerning various areas of opera and opera performance. The most popular operas are covered in more depth than are the little known ones.

Groves Dictionary of Music and Musicians. Eric Blom, ed. New York: St. Martin's, 1970.

This "Bible of Music" is encyclopedic in nature. It covers the period from 1450 to the present and contains, among other items, biographical material on musicians and patrons of music; definitions of musical terms; origin, structure and modifications of instruments; and histories of musical societies and institutions.

Harvard Dictionary of Music. Willi Apel. Cambridge: Harvard Univ. Press, 1970.

One of the most valuable reference books in the musical field, it includes no biographical articles, but concentrates on the historical point of view. Definitions cover a wide range of musical topics, concentrating on compositional techniques and including such new areas as electronic and serial music. Representative compositions of every type from every era are covered. There are bibliographies after each article, as well as illustrations, charts, diagrams, musical examples, and a list of music libraries and their holdings.

Music Index. Detroit: Information Service, 1949—.

Author, title and subject index using titles of vocal works, book and performance reviews and geographical headings as major categories. Some foreign periodicals are indexed. It is published monthly and has annual cumulations.

Philosophy

The Concise Encyclopedia of Western Philosophy and Philosophers. J. O. Urmson, ed. New York: Hawthorn Books, 1960.

Major philosophical terms, schools, and men described in articles that cover philosophy from ancient Greece to present.

Dictionary of Philosophy and Psychology. James M. Baldwin, ed. New York: Macmillan, 1901-1905.

Limited though it is to an early Twentieth-century view of philosophy and psychology, this compendium of short articles provides etymologies of terms; glossaries in English, French, German and Italian; bibliography of philosophers' works—as well as articles by such leading philosophers as John Dewey and Charles Peirce.

Encyclopedia of Philosophy. Paul Edwards, ed. New York: Macmillan, 1967.

For a close, clear explanation of any branch of philosophy this authoritative eight-volume work covers not only the mainstream, but also the tributaries of philosophical thought (mathematics, religion, sociology, etc.). Excellent bibliographies follow each article.

Great Books of the Western World and *The Great Ideas, a Syntopticon.* Mortimer J. Adler, ed. Chicago: Encyclopedia Britannica, 1961.

The two-volume *Syntopticon* contains an analytic essay for each of the 102 "great ideas." Under "law," for instance, there is a clear and succinct approach to the divine and natural law, and the relationship of law and the individual. The remaining fifty-four volumes contain the works of the great thinkers and writers of Western civilization. To these fifty-four volumes the essays of the *Syntopticon* are keyed, permitting one to trace the development of an idea through history or to compare the views of two or more giants of history. Each of the 102 essays is cross-indexed, providing innumerable approaches to a single subject.

A History of Philosophy. 7 vols. Frederick Copleston. New York: Image Books, Doubleday, 1960-1964.

From the Pre-Socratics up to Nietzsche, Copleston carefully summarizes the lives and thoughts of major figures while providing a scholarly story. Especially good treatment of the major Greek and medieval philosophers, rationalism in the seventeenth-century, and Kant.

Masterpieces of World Philosophy in Summary Form. Frank N. Magill, ed. New York: Harper & Row, 1963.

Some academicians feel that students of philosophy or political theory must gain their understanding from the original works of the philosophers themselves with little or no outside assistance. There is room for disagreement. While it is always beneficial to read the original, most students can help sharpen their understanding with outside direction. A glance at one of the summaries offered in this volume is likely to raise the student's level of comprehension. Also, there are times when it is neither wise nor possible to read an entire work, in which case this reference can save the day.

Psychology

A Bibliography of Theory and Research Techniques in the Field of Human Motivation. New York: Advertising Research Foundation, 1956.

Annotated bibliography on techniques, application, and theory of research in the field of motivational research.

*A Comprehensive Dictionary of Psychological and Psychoana-
lytical Terms.* Horace B. English, and Ava C. English, eds.
London: Longmans, Green, 1958.

Contemporary dictionary covering a wide field. The definitions are brief and not meant to paint an historical picture.
Besides being quotable, it provides a useful summary of concepts such as "childhood."

Dictionary of Philosophy and Psychology. See page 98.

Psychological Abstracts. Washington, D.C.: American Psychological Assoc., 1936—.

Takes the place of, but is less inclusive than, the *Psychological Index.* It contains abstracts or summaries of articles and
books in the field of psychology and appears bi-monthly with
cumulations. If a speaker is interested in topics such as color
psychology or why certain advertisements are effective, this
source could lead him to case studies or test data that could
support contentions planned for the speech.

Psychological Index. Princeton, N.J.: Psychological Review Co.

This source, which is arranged according to subject,
indexes books and periodical articles in the field of psychology
from 1895-1936. It was replaced by *Psychological Abstracts.*

Religion and Mythology

Curiosities of Popular Custom. William S. Walsh. Philadelphia:
Lippincott, 1898.

Frequently reprinted reference work including much information concerning rites, ceremonies, church holidays, saints,
and the histories of various customs and their celebrations.
Much of this subject matter is omitted from regular references.
It is arranged alphabetically but lacks table of contents and
cross-references.

Encyclopaedia of Religion and Ethics. James Hastings, et al., eds. New York: Scribner's, 1908-1927.

Thirteen-volume set that contains medium length to chapter-length essays dealing with all the religions, their theologies, philosophies, dates, vocabularies, and saints. A scholarly, fairly detailed place to go when comparing theologies. One volume is devoted to a complete subject and article index.

Encyclopedia of Superstitions. Rev. ed. Christina Hole, ed. London: Hutchinson, 1961.

Popular work including superstitions, mostly of British origin, which are individually classified with title headings in order to quickly obtain a list of beliefs attached to any subject — and the origin of the belief. Customs of which the origin is unknown are omitted. There is a bibliography, but no index; and it is sometimes difficult to tell under what subject a superstition has been classified.

Funk and Wagnall's Standard Dictionary of Folklore, Mythology and Legend. Maria Leach, ed. New York: Funk and Wagnalls, 1949-50.

Two-volume work arranged alphabetically which, though incomplete, contains a worthwhile sampling of information concerning gods, heroes, customs, witchcraft, the occult, and especially folklore and legend.

Man, Myth and Magic: An Illustrated Encyclopedia of the Supernatural. Richard Cavendish, ed. New York: Marshall Cavendish, 1970.

The Editorial Board and contributors of this twenty-four volume set are made up of experts either in the particular area that their article covers or in anthropology. It contains short articles, arranged for the most part alphabetically, that deal with the particular belief or idea historically and then, toward the end, there is usually some attempt at evaluation and criticism. Myths and beliefs from all over the world are included, as are Christian concepts and symbols. Illustrations are mostly in color and increase the interest value of this set of books to the point that any speech student's creativity should be inspired considerably. For this reason, it will be especially useful for those students having a difficult time finding a speech topic. Also, in order to lead the student to other sources, short bibliographies are often included after the articles. The last volume presents a comprehensive bibliography and subject headings with the related articles in the set listed under them.

New Catholic Encyclopedia. 15 vols. William J. McDonald, ed. in chief. New York: McGraw-Hill, 1967.

Ecumenical in spirit, it presents Catholicism and the world in all their relations. Both ecclesiastical matters and general articles on religions, institutions, persons, scientific developments, philosophies, and movements that have affected Catholicism are written from a Catholic viewpoint.

New Schaff-Herzog Encyclopedia of Religion. Philip Schaff. Grand Rapids, Mich.: Baker Book House, 1950.

Thirteen-volume set that covers all aspects of religious and theological knowledge in a factual, unbiased manner from earliest times to 1908. It emphasizes Christianity and Protestantism, and includes biographies of religious leaders with emphasis on their religious thoughts and contributions. Also a source for excellent bibliographies.

Universal Jewish Encyclopedia. 11 vols. Isaac Landman, et al. New York: Universal Jewish Encyclopedia, Inc., 1939-1944.

The history of the Jews and Judaism from the earliest times is given in signed articles with selected bibliographies. American developments are well-covered. Volume 11 presents a guide of 100 outlines grouping the major articles under seven headings with references to the appropriate articles.

Science, Engineering, Mathematics, Agriculture

Biological and Agricultural Index. New York: H. W. Wilson, 1964–. Monthly.

Formerly the *Agricultural Index*, it is a subject index to the contents of periodicals, books, bulletins, pamphlets, and reports in the areas of agricultural chemicals, bacteriology, botany, ecology, entomology, farm economics, forestry, horticulture, rural sociology, veterinary science, zoology, and soil science. Comes out monthly, except September, and has annual cumulations.

Encyclopedia of Biological Science. Peter Grey, ed. New York: Reinhold, 1961.

Provides brief, accurate information for both non-biologists and biologists in fields where they are not experts. The articles deal with pure biological science, not with bio-chemistry, and each article is signed and followed by a bibliography. The reference work contains an index and many illustrations.

International Dictionary of Physics and Electronics. Walter D. Michels, ed. New York: Van Nostrand, 1961.

The introduction of this reference work gives the non-physicist background information and basic concepts, while the body of the dictionary contains specific terminology and omits articles that would be uninteresting to the professional physicist. It is arranged alphabetically, illustrated and indexed in English, Spanish, German, and Russian. A speaker must gauge his audience carefully before becoming too detailed and technical, so care must be used with this reference guide as well as the others in specialized areas.

Larousse Encyclopedia of Astronomy. Lucien Rudaux. New York: Prometheus Press, 1959.

Provides basic information in astronomy that can serve as a background for more detailed study in special areas. It includes an index, plates, tables, and other illustrations.

McGraw-Hill Encyclopedia of Science and Technology. New York: McGraw-Hill, 1966.

Provides a wide range of understandable material in the natural sciences and all their applications in engineering, agriculture, forestry, industrial biology, food, and other areas. Basic information is also included in anatomy, embryology and bio-chemistry. It is both indexed and illustrated.

Putnam's Nature Series. New York: Putnam, various dates.

Series of individually edited, fairly comprehensive, compact books that deal with all types of birds, fish, mammals, wild flowers, ferns, rocks and minerals, insects, trees and shrubs, seashore life, rivers and streams, stars, skies, shells, snakes, mushrooms, and nature activities in general. Each book has many excellent illustrations and is designed to be the source of identification for the subject of the title—so it is good to carry on field trips. They all cover non-technical questions that might be asked by the amateur.

Van Nostrand's Scientific Encyclopedia. New York: Van Nostrand, 1968.

Probably the best one-volume scientific encyclopedia. Each article becomes progressively more detailed and technical. It is cross-referenced and profusely illustrated.

Social Sciences

GENERAL WORKS
Current Digest of the Soviet Press. The American Association for the Advancement of Slavic Studies. Columbus, Ohio: Ohio State University Press, 1929—.

Next to being there, this publication is considered one of the best ways to study the Soviet Union. Each week it publishes American translations of all the major documents and significant articles from about sixty Soviet newspapers and magazines, plus a complete index to the two principal dailies, *Pravda* and *Izvestia.* The translations are presented without comment or even interpretation. They provide excellent raw material for critical analysis done under the watchful eye of an experienced teacher. A detailed quarterly index is also published as is a new monthly, *Current Abstracts of the Soviet Press,* offering, obviously, the monthly highlights of Soviet news with emphasis on internal discussion.

A Dictionary of the Social Sciences. Julius Gould and W. L. Kolb, eds. New York: The Free Press of Glencoe, 1964.

For both the meanings of terms and the historical backgrounds, this volume provides brief, general information in the areas of sociology, political science, economics, social anthropology and social psychology. Published under the auspices of UNESCO.

Encyclopedia of the Social Sciences. E. R. A. Seligman, ed. New York: Crowell-Collier and Macmillan, 1930-1935.

Hundreds of international scholars prepared this comprehensive survey of the fields of social science in the early 1930's. They have produced a work that is considered to be the most important in this field. Somewhat out-of-date today, it should be used with the newer *International Encyclopedia of Social Sciences,* though the editors of the newer work did not intend to supercede the older volumes. This set contains many classic articles by leading social scientists, articles that helped to define an entire field of study. The seventeen volumes include a 349-page introduction in two parts: a discussion of the meaning of the social sciences and an outline of their chronological development, and a nation-by-nation survey of the disciplines involved in the social sciences. The main portion of the work deals with the important concepts in political sciences, economics, law, anthropology, sociology, penology, and social work. About a quarter of the work is composed of biographical sketches. All entries are alphabetically arranged with cross references and a subject index.

International Yearbook and Statesmen's Who's Who. London: Burke's Peerage, 1953—.

Combines data on political and economic conditions of the world with an international biographical directory of about 10,000 individuals of world renown: statesmen, diplomats, military leaders, clergy, industrialists, and so forth. The information on various nations, arranged alphabetically, is similar to that in the *Statesman's Yearbook* but with more statistical details.

*Issues before the General Assemblies of the United Nations:
1946-1965.* New York: Arno, 1970.

A specially compiled selection of excerpts from the major
speeches and issues on the General Assembly agenda since its
first session in 1946. Also compiled for this edition is a cumulative index that allows the student to find in one source basic
information concerning relevant problems facing the United
Nations.

Public Affairs Information Service Index. New York: Public
Affairs Information Service, Inc., 1915—.

Index, with annual cumulations, that unifies a wide variety
of sources concerned with public affairs. Besides periodicals it
lists books, pamphlets, and government documents. The subjects include economics, social conditions, politics, and international relations. Its bibliography is adequate for identification,
and most articles include brief explanatory items.

Reader's Guide to the Social Sciences. Bert F. Hoselitz, ed.
Glencoe, Illinois: The Free Press, 1959—.

This is divided into sections of history, geography, sociology, anthropology, psychology, economics and political science. The last chapter is written by Heinz Eulau, who presents a
splendid introduction to the more important studies in political
science.

*Sources of Information in the Social Sciences: A Guide to the
Literature.* Carl M. White, et al. Totowa, N.J.: The Bedminster
Press, 1964.

Besides general reference works, this source offers a separate treatment to history, economics and business administration, sociology, anthropology, psychology, education, and
political science. Each chapter is complete with introduction,
important studies, bibliographies, and data sources. The volume
is geared for the interdisciplinary and behavioral approach to
the social sciences.

Statesman's Year Book: Statistical and Historical Annual of the States of the World. John Paxton, ed. New York: St. Martin's, 1864–.

A general yearbook of more than general value, this book offers a yearly update of economic, political, and social statistics and information on the major international organizations, and on every nation during the preceding year. The data include each nation's constitution, political and governmental structure, financial basis, gross national product, court system, etc.

Statistical Abstract for Latin America. Berkeley, Calif.: University of California Press, 1956–.

This volume, which is issued annually, presents current statistical data on all Latin American nations and their dependencies. Information is offered on area, population, social organization, economic characteristics, finances, foreign trade, and other special topics. Notes and source information accompany its tables; it contains an adequate bibliography.

Statistical Abstract of the United States. Washington, D.C.: Government Printing Office 1879–.

Published annually, this work is a recognized, reliable summary of statistics on the social, political, and economic organization of the United States. It also serves as a guide to other statistical publications and sources through the introductory text to each section, the source notes for each table, and the bibliography of sources. Here one can find information of primarily national concern. Also included are many tables for regions and individual states and statistics for the commonwealth of Puerto Rico and other outlying areas of the United States.

Additional information for cities, counties, metropolitan areas, congressional districts, and other small units is available in supplements to the abstract (such as *County and City Data Book*; *Congressional District Data Book*; *Historical Statistics of the U.S., Colonial Times to 1957*; and *Historical Statistics of the U.S., Colonial Times to 1957, Continuation to 1962 and Revisions*). The *Statistical Abstract* is the most reliable source for such data as births; deaths; marriages and divorces; number of physicians, dentists, and nurses; immigration and naturalization; law enforcement, courts, and prisons; geography and climate; public lands and parks; recreation and travel; elections; and incomes.

United Nations Statistical Yearbook. New York: United Nations Statistical Office, 1949—.

A continuation of the *Statistical Yearbook of the League of Nations, 1927-1945.* The upheaval of World War II caused the gap between 1945 and 1949. Its tables cover world population, man-power, agriculture, production, mining construction, consumption, transportation, external trade, wages, prices, national income, finance, social statistics, education, and culture. A ten-to-twenty-year period is generally given for each series. Its sources are cited, it contains subject and nation indexes, and its text is written in French and English. Current data for many tables are published regularly by the United Nations Statistical Office *Monthly Bulletin of Statistics* (which has been in existence since 1947).

GEOGRAPHY
Columbia Lippincott Gazeteer of the World. Leon E. Seltzer, ed. New York: Columbia University Press, 1962. Supplements.

This comprehensive collection of data ranges over all the globe, giving politico-geographical and cultural facts about each country or area.

Webster's New Geographical Dictionary. Springfield, Mass.: Merriam, 1972.

Provides, in a single alphabetically arranged volume, a large selection of geographical proper names along with spelling, pronunciation, geographical and, occasionally, historical information, and maps.

HISTORY

Dictionary of American History. James T. Adams, ed. New York: Scribner's, Vols. 1-6, 1944; supplement, 1961; vol. 7, 1963.

Gives short, concise answers to specific questions on American history such as events, trends or policies. Each article is signed and has a bibliography. Its index is arranged alphabetically. Since it was conceived as a companion to the *Dictionary of American Biography*, it contains no biographies.

An Encyclopedia of World History. William L. Langer, ed. Boston: Houghton Mifflin, 1968.

In no other volume can one locate the essential facts of world history so quickly. Using an expanded outline form with important names and dates in boldface type, this single volume covers the recorded history of the world. Extensively indexed, it allows one to spend a minimum of effort in finding such data as the chronology of the short Soviet-Finno war of 1939-1940, or the Muslim conquest of Spain.

Historical Statistics of the United States, Colonial Times to 1957. Washington, D.C.: Government Printing Office, 1960.

Supplement to the *Statistical Abstract of the United States*, which contains more than 8,000 statistical studies grouped mostly into yearly periods. It covers economic and social development from 1610 to 1957 and includes definitions of terms and descriptive text. Source notes provide a guide for students who wish to read the original published sources for further reference and data. It contains a complete subject index alphabetically arranged. The work also includes about 300 series that are complements to or substitutes for any series discontinued since 1956.

POLITICAL SCIENCE

Almanac of Current World Leaders. Los Angeles, Calif.: Almanac of Current World Leaders, 1959—.

Brief biographies of world leaders in the current news. Special note is taken of those nations in which leadership has changed since the last publication (which is quarterly). Also lists, by nation, heads of state, cabinet ministers, and their political affiliations; as well as a chronological listing of events involving changes in governmental and other important posts.

Book of the States. Chicago: Council of State Governments, 1935—.

This biennial is a rich source of authoritative information on the actual structure, working methods, functioning, and financing of state governments. The legislative, executive, and judicial branches are outlined in depth according to their inter-governmental relations and the major areas of public service performed by each. The 1970-1971 edition has two supplements, which list the state officials and legislators.

Important statistics are also contained in these volumes; salaries and compensations of state legislators, divorce laws, voting laws and regulations, state departments, welfare budgets and payments, and educational salaries and budgets.

Congressional Digest. Washington, D.C.: Congressional Digest Corporation, 1921—.

Privately printed monthly publication that explores both sides of current controversial topics. After an opening statement of the question under discussion, pro and con arguments drawn from the opinions of world experts in that particular field are advanced.

Congressional Directory. Washington, D.C.: Government Printing Office, 1809—.

Directory, which appears with every session of Congress, contains information on United States congressmen. Each congressman is given a limited number of free copies to distribute to his constituents. The directory contains short biographical sketches of every member of both houses. It also lists the membership of each congressional committee and outlines the committee assignments given each member. One may locate here the name of his congressman, a brief sketch of his life, the boundaries of the voting district in which he lives, and his margin of victory in the last several elections.

Also listed are the major executives of every government agency, as are members of the diplomatic corps, and members of the press who have accredited seating in the congressional press galleries. A pocket edition of this directory contains a photograph of each member of Congress, but omits other information.

Congressional Quarterly Service

Although privately printed since 1945, the "CQ" series of publications has achieved the status of an official publication and is the most frequently cited source of congressional information. Its major attribute is its concise factual arrangement of material previously tucked away in bulky government documents.

The Congressional Quarterly publications present a careful review of each session of Congress in both legislative and political areas. Facts, figures, and unbiased commentary on all aspects of congressional activity are presented, including committee meetings and floor action. The president's position on all major legislation and rollcall votes in Congress are included, as are the president's messages to Congress, his news conferences, his vetoes, and so on.

The basic publication of the service is the *Congressional Quarterly Weekly Report.* From this report a yearly *Congressional Quarterly Almanac* is compiled.

Congress and the Nation is a hard-bound volume documenting all major congressional and presidential actions and national political campaigns for the twenty-year period from 1945 to 1964. Volume II, covering the Johnson years (1965-1968), was published in 1969.

Congressional Quarterly also publishes semiannually a current handbook for the study of American government, the *Congressional Quarterly Guide to Current American Government,* which contains research material written and arranged for classroom and study use, as well as the *Editorial Research Reports,* a weekly publication that objectively assembles the facts involved in current controversial topics in well-researched and documented articles of about 6,000 words each. A library subscribing to the *Congressional Quarterly Weekly Report* probably also receives the *Editorial Research Reports.*

Congressional Record. Washington, D.C.: Government Printing Office, 1873—.

The *Record* is a nearly verbatim account of everything uttered aloud on the floor of Congress, as well as of some material not actually spoken but entered as an "extension of remarks." It is published Monday through Friday when Congress is in session. The *Congressional Record* is a valuable source because congressmen frequently insert letters and articles that are in themselves primary sources of information on topics under discussion.

Prior to 1873 the *Congressional Record* was titled *Congressional Globe* (1833-1873); before that it was called *The Register of Debates* (1824-1837); and even earlier, *Annals of Congress* (1789-1824). It is cataloged under these titles in libraries. Each set consists of fifteen to twenty parts a year, including a separate index. In 1947 the *Daily Digest* volumes were added, which review highlights, list scheduled hearings of Congress, and summarize day-to-day committee activity.

The *Congressional Record* contains a two-part index, consisting of an alphabetical listing of subjects and names and a history of bills and resolutions arranged by their numbers. This second section is thought to be the best available source for tracing the route of a particular bill. Because this is a daily record, the best method of locating information is first to establish the date on which the debate took place.

A student may request his congressman to put his name on the mailing list for the Congressional Record. It is a free service rendered by congressmen to their constituents. However, unless the student is willing to read and digest some 200 pages a day, this would be wasteful, as each congressman's subscriptions are limited.

Congressional Serial Set. Washington, D.C.: Government Printing Office, 1817—.

This set of 13,500 volumes is a collection of documents containing House and Senate journals, documents, and reports. It does not include bills, hearings, laws, or "committee prints." The reports are committee reports and are especially important in that they contain not only brief summaries of the hearings, but also the individual views of the committee members who participated. Committee reports usually contain the best brief summary of all the important facts and arguments related to the bill in question.

Obviously, it can be difficult to trace a document through 13,500 volumes, so the following indexes, all published by the Government Printing Office, can help one find a particular item.

Checklist of United States Public Documents, 1789-1909. (Washington, D.C.: Government Printing Office, 1911. Reprinted, New York: Kraus Reprint Co., 1962).

Catalog of the Public Documents of Congress, 1893-1940. (Washington, D.C.: Government Printing Office). Published irregularly between 1896 and 1945.

Decennial Cumulative Index 1941-1950. 25 vols. (Washington, D.C.: Government Printing Office, 1953). Succeeded by an index series published yearly.

Numerical Lists and Schedules of Volumes of the Reports and Documents for each session of Congress. First published for the seventy-third Congress (1933-1934), published biennially thereafter.

The Monthly Catalog of United States Government Publications lists most of the volumes as they are sent to the depository libraries, and is, itself, sent to each library as an index. These "depository libraries" are usually the state universities in the larger cities of every state.

Deadline Data on World Affairs. Greenwich, Conn.: Deadline Data, 1956—.

Published four times a month on 5 X 8-inch file cards, the data are arranged alphabetically by country and sub-filed under "general," "domestic" or "foreign policy" categories. Occasionally something is filed by subject, such as "selective service." Since 1968 a compilation of this data into monthly reports called *On Record* has been published. This is an especially useful source for a quick summary or chronology of a recent political event.

Department of State Bulletin. Washington, D.C.: Government Printing Office.

Up-to-date information on international relations and the official administration view of American foreign policy. Published weekly, it contains messages delivered by the president and speeches delivered by other U.S. officials. It also fills its columns with State Department press releases, terms of new treaties, and analyses of current foreign policy issues.

Everyman's United Nations. New York: United Nations Department of Public Information, 1968.

Primary source for the structure, functions, and work of the United Nations and its related agencies. This frequently revised handbook is divided into four parts: Part I discusses the organization of the United Nations; Part II is concerned with political, social, economic, and security questions; Part III deals with specialized agencies, such as the Food and Agriculture Organization (FAO), the United Nations Educational, Scientific, and Cultural Organization (UNESCO), and many others; Part IV gives an index, the chronology, and a list of the United Nations Information Centers.

Guide to the Study of International Relations. J. K. Zawodny. San Francisco: Chandler, 1966.

Paperback guide designed to aid the student and researcher in finding the widely scattered and often complex materials tied to the study of international relations—government documents, national archives, UN publications, and up-to-date, empirically validated findings in the behavioral sciences. It has more than 500 cross-indexed entries classified under subject headings which, except for the journals, have been annotated and can guide the student efficiently through several million titles to the specific ones he desires.

Municipal Yearbook. Chicago: International City Managers' Association, 1934–.

As an annual reference, it is certainly the best source in its field. It is an authoritative resume of activities and statistical data of American cities, with emphasis on individual city programs. Attention is devoted to developments in urban counties and metropolitan areas. One can also find in it thorough bibliographies and comprehensive directories of officials.

National Journal. Cliff Sessions, ed. Washington, D.C.: Center for Political Research, 1970–.

Journal founded by a group of editors and reporters who left *Congressional Quarterly* because they felt it did not pay enough attention to bureaucratic decision-making. The *Journal* is published weekly and designed as a monitor of all government actions. It does more than record government action; it analyzes all the details surrounding such actions, focusing mainly on the relationships between the various power-wielding agencies that cram the nation's capital. The interests involved in any issue are plainly identified—this, in itself, cuts away much that might be arcane to the student. It also contains in-depth reports on federal programs, biographical information on government officials, and analyses of congressional districts.

National Party Platforms 1840-1970. Kirk Porter and Donald Johnson. Urbana: University of Illinois Press. With supplements.

Even though a political party platform is not often followed after elections, it must be considered as an indicator of the goals and internal dissensions of the party. Included are the platforms of many minor parties, as well as the two major parties. In 1960, for example, this work included the platforms of Democratic, Republican, Prohibition Socialist, Socialist, Labor, and Socialist Worker parties.

United States Code & United States Statutes At Large. Washington, D.C.: Government Printing Office, 1875–.

The *United States Code* is published every six years, with an annual supplement. This is the source to consult for a speech on any legislation that has been passed by Congress. It is the source of up-to-date public laws covering every topic. Another source for public laws is *United States Statutes At Large,* which divides the public laws into two parts: first, all public laws that were passed during a particular year; and second, all private bills passed. Laws in both books are classified under fifty titles, such as public lands, education, defense, Congress, and banks.

There are also commercially published editions of this work known as *United States Code Annotated* (St. Paul, Minn.: West Publishing Company, 1927–) and *Federal Code Annotated* (New York & Indianapolis, Ind.: Bobbs-Merrill Company, 1937–). These annotated editions include notes on judicial interpretations of the law as well as the law itself. If available, they are more useful than the *United States Code.*

If one is interested in state rather than federal laws, the proper source would, of course, be individual state codes.

United States Government Organization Manual. Washington, D.C.: Government Printing Office, 1935–.

Annually published study that is the prime source for the current organization and functions of each of the departments and agencies that make up the executive branch. It is the official organization handbook of the federal government and contains sections describing the agencies of the legislative, judicial, and executive branches. It also presents brief descriptions of quasi-official agencies and of selected international organizations. This manual may serve as a source of ideas for speeches about governmental reorganization and efficiency.

United States in World Affairs. The Council on Foreign Relations. New York: Harper & Row, 1967—.

Published yearly, this book is a series of interpretive essays that try to explain American foreign policy. A detailed chronology in the appendix makes this series most useful as an integrator of events. For example, the contents for 1966 list: "What Price a Free Vietnam"; "Origins of the Problem's Two Views"; "End of the Pause"; "Honolulu and After"; "The Debate Continues and So Does the War."

Weekly Compilation of Presidential Documents. Washington, D.C.: Government Printing Office, 1965—.

Published every Monday under the auspices of the Office of the Federal Register, National Archives and Records Service, and General Services Administration, this source contains the presidential materials released by the White House up to 5 P.M. the preceding Friday. It includes the president's addresses, remarks, announcements, appointments and nominations, executive orders, memoranda, meetings with foreign leaders, and proclamations, as well as reports to the president.

Yearbook of the United Nations. New York: United Nations Department of Public Information, 1947—.

Annual editions constitute a year-by-year record of the activities of the United Nations. Each edition is designed to present within a single, fully indexed volume a compact authoritative account of the deliberations and actions of the United Nations, as well as the activities of the intergovernmental agencies related to it.

SOCIOLOGY

Encyclopedia of Social Work. H. L. Lurie, ed. New York: National Association of Social Workers, 1929—.

Previous to 1965, known as the *Social Work Year Book,* this collection of current research includes history, statistics, biographies of past leaders in the U.S. and Canada, a directory of agencies and some information on social work in other nations. The signed articles contain current bibliographies.

Handbook of Modern Sociology. Robert E. L. Faris, ed. Chicago: Rand McNally, 1964.

Series of essays covering twenty-seven broad areas of sociology spotlighting fairly current research. Charts and tables are provided. It is a good source for examining the behavior of major societies.

International Bibliography of Sociology. International Sociological Association. Chicago: Aldine, 1952—.

Published annually, this major work divides its subject into six sections: History and Organization of Social Studies, Theories and Methods of Sociology, Social Structure, Social Control and Communication, Social Change, Social Problems and Social Policy. The index is a worldwide list of authors and subjects. One of the first sources to go to for speeches on the field.

Negro Yearbook. Jessie Guzman, ed. New York: Wise, 1952. Irregular.

Presents such current facts concerning American Negroes as population statistics, education, religious information, business, politics, housing, crime, health, sports, professions, books, motion pictures, song writers, periodicals, and organizations. It contains an index to both names and subjects.

Sociological Abstracts. Leo P. Chall, ed. New York: Sociological Abstracts, Inc., 1952—.

Usually published eight times a year with a cumulative index, the abstracts are short summaries of articles or books published anywhere in the world. Subject headings and sub-classifications make it easy to find works. It permits the student to determine quickly if a book is the one he needs.

Social Work Year Book. Russell Kurtz, ed. New York: National Association of Social Workers, 1929-1965.

Appearing biennially, it covers mostly U.S. organizations and consists of three parts: first, articles on history, status and trends; second, topical articles on adoption, alcoholism, youth services, disaster relief, etc.; third, a directory of international and national agencies. It contains an analytical index and each edition is independent of previous editions.

Theater, Cinema, Dance

Best Plays of [Various Years]. New York: Dodd, Mead, 1894–.

Contains summaries of the theater seasons in New York, London, Paris and other cities of the world. It includes details of the reception; statistics regarding plays; award winners; books on the theater; an index of authors, plays, and casts, producers, directors, designers, etc.; many illustrations; and a list of the ten best plays with summaries and key scenes of these plays. It was formerly edited by Burns Mantle, but is now under various editors.

Cumulated Dramatic Index, 1909-1949. Boston, Mass.: G. K. Hall, 1965.

Cumulation of the F. W. Faxon Company's *Dramatic Index*. It is arranged under subjects, titles, playwrights, and famous characters and is limited to English works of the U.S. and Great Britain, but includes foreign plays. It is an excellent source of illustrations and reviews of productions as well as to biographical information.

Drama Criticism. Volume II: A Checklist of Interpretation Since 1940 of Classical and Continental Plays. Arthur Coleman and Gary Tyler. Chicago: Swallow Press, 1969.

Volume II completes the coverage of interpretation since 1940 of British and American plays. As in the first volume, the entries are arranged by author and then by play. It will supplement *American Drama Criticism: Interpretations, 1890-1965 Inclusive of American Drama Since the First Play Produced in America* (Archon, 1967) and *Modern Drama: a Checklist of Critical Literature on 20th Century Plays* (Scarecrow, 1967). For any student interested in giving a speech dealing with dramatic and literary criticism, this two-volume set should prove useful.

A History of the Theatre. George Freedley and John A. Reeves. New York: Crown, 1955.

With its supplementary section this volume lists essays, playwrights, plays, actors, and playhouses of "legitimate" drama from the early Egyptian and Greek theaters up to the mid-twentieth century.

Index to One-Act Plays. Hannah Logasa and Ver Nooy. Boston: Faxon, 1924. Latest supplement, 1966.

This latest supplement indexes plays from 1900 to 1964 that were written or translated into English and those published in collections, periodicals, or as separate pamphlets, as well as radio plays and plays for children.

Index to Plays 1800-1926. Ina Firkins. New York: H. W. Wilson, 1927. Latest supplements, 1935.

Both of these play indexes are arranged according to authors, subjects, and titles. Well-known plays rather than artistically worthy plays are listed. Includes plot summaries, bibliographical information, types and number of characters, length of playing time and, often, the suitability for particular audiences.

Modern World Drama. Myron Matlaw. New York: Dutton, Inc., 1972.

Only reference work in drama covering the period from mid-19th century to present, it is arranged alphabetically and profusely illustrated. Entries for each dramatic work include plot synopses, factual data, historical and critical notes. Latin America and West Africa are included in the geographical areas, and various ethnic entries are also included. All of the recent theatrical movements are covered and every entry has a bibliography. Two indexes, the "Character Index" and the "General Index," list characters in the modern plays, playwrights, dramatic works, technical terms, and geographical areas of the modern world.

Oxford Companion to the Theatre. Phyllis Hartnoll, ed. New York: Oxford University Press, 1967.

Well-illustrated handbook that is especially good for theater history rather than for the literary aspects of drams. It contains short alphabetically arranged articles on major actors, directors, designers, and playwrights from both the past and present. Also includes articles on ballet and music, and traces many theatrical developments and styles. Good basic bibliographies are included and the contributors are listed, but no index or table of contents is added, which is a drawback, since group headings are used.

Play Index, 1949—. Estelle A. Fidell. New York: H. W. Wilson, 1968.

A three-volume index, it includes author, title, and subject indexes; a list of collections indexed; cast analyses; a directory of publishers; a wide variety of playwrights, play summaries, and play types, including those for children and puppets.

The Reader's Encyclopedia of World Drama. John Gassner and Edward Quin, eds. New York: Crowell, 1969.

Designed as a readable and ready source for the general audience of those interested in theater, this one-volume work concentrates on drama more as literature than as theater. Therefore, focus rests upon plays, playwrights, and literary characteristics. In this way it helps fill in the gaps left by the *Oxford Companion to the Theatre.* Entries fall into four main categories. First, national drama, which contains under the country's name a historical survey of the development of that nation's drama from earliest to contemporary times. Usually bibliographies of mostly English works are attached. Second, the significant playwrights are cited along with biographical sketches, important works and critical evaluations. Third, a category that covers plays, a summary of the main action and critical commentary. And fourth, all the major dramatic modes and several minor ones are discussed. All articles are signed with the initials of about 95 contributors. Basic documents in dramatic theory are found in an appendix but, unfortunately, there is no index.

Theatre and Allied Arts. Blanche Baker. New York: H. W. Wilson, 1966.

This alphabetically arranged handbook is a descriptive list of books dealing with the history, criticism, and techniques of drama and its related crafts and arts. Its three sections consist of the following: first, drama, theater, and actors; second, stagecraft; third, miscellaneous. No information is listed for radio, television, motion pictures, or opera. It does have an author and subject index, and is slanted toward the U.S.

CINEMA
International Motion Picture Almanac. Charles Aaronson. New York: Quigley, 1929–.

This annual publication contains the answer to almost any question concerning the motion picture industry or people connected with it. It includes a who's who, biographies, suppliers, producers, etc. It is indexed and contains a table of contents that divides the book into different subject areas, which are slanted toward the U.S.

International Television Almanac. 1956–.

It has the same author, publisher, and coverage of the television world as in *The International Motion Picture Almanac,* to which it is a companion publication.

DANCE
Dance Encyclopedia. Anatole Chujoy and P. W. Manchester. New York: Barnes, 1949. Rev. & enlarged by Simon & Schuster, 1967.

Reference source that combines the history, science, and tradition of dance. It includes a large bibliography of books on the dance and a list of records of theater dance music. It also contains definitions of pertinent terms, biographical sketches, and articles by specialists.

REFERENCE MATERIAL IN THE FIELD OF SPEECH

General Speech

Bibliographies
Baird, Albert Craig. "A Selected Bibliography of American Oratory," *Quarterly Journal of Speech,* XII (1926), 352-56.

Useful bibliography for the beginning student which will lead him to collections of American speeches and to books about the speakers.

Bibliographic Annual in Speech Communication. Ned A. Shearer, ed. New York: Speech Communication Association, 1970.

A great benefit to anyone doing research in the area of speech communication, bibliographies that were previously published in various periodicals (and are listed as such in this section) are now found in this yearly publication. The following bibliographies are included: "A Bibliography of Rhetoric and Public Address for the Year ⸺ ," previously published in *Quarterly Journal of Speech* and *Speech Monographs*; "Doctoral Dissertations in Speech Communication: Work in Progress"; "Abstracts of Doctoral Dissertations in the Field of Speech Communication," 1969–; "Graduate Theses and Dissertation Titles: An Index of Graduate Research in Speech Communication," 1969–; "Bibliography of American Elocution"; and at times special bibliographies of noted speakers are included.

"A Bibliography of Rhetoric and Public Address for the Year (1947–)," *Quarterly Journal of Speech,* XXXIV. (1948–) XXXVI (1950), *Speech Monographs,* XVIII (1951-1969). Ed. successively by Frederick W. Haberman and J. W. Cleary.

Probably the most comprehensive bibliography of current work in the history, theory, and criticism of public address. Also deals somewhat with radio and television, discussion and debate and with various experimental studies in these areas. The bibliographies appear annually in the first section. It is now, as of 1970, published in the *Bibliographic Annual in Speech Communication,* listed above.

Brockett, O. G., and others. *A Bibliographical Guide to Research in Speech and Dramatic Art.* Chicago: Scott, Foresman, 1963.

Comprehensive in its approach and slanted toward works in English, it also includes major references and works in other languages. This compact book includes not only one of the most complete lists of reference works in the field of speech and theater, but also all types of useful general references and those areas from allied fields that could be helpful to speech and theater students. The allied arts section includes education, art, aesthetics, dance, music, history and politics, literature, psychology, law, sociology, and anthropology. It is annotated, but in some cases the annotations need to be expanded just a little in order to be useful to an undergraduate student.

Cleary, James W., and Haberman, Frederick W. *Rhetoric and Public Address: A Bibliography, 1947-1961.* Madison and Milwaukee, 1964.

Corrections, omissions, and additions to the annual bibliographies published in the *Quarterly Journal of Speech,* 1947-51, and in *Speech Monographs,* 1952-61, resulted in this alphabetically arranged reference source. It has a subject index, a list of practitioners and theorists, and an index of reviewers. *The Bibliography of Rhetoric and Public Address,* which appears annually in *Speech Monographs* is a continuation of it.

Duker, Sam. *A Bibliography on Listening.* Brooklyn, New York: Brooklyn College, Office of Testing and Research, 1961.

Because it is so important for the speaker to understand the problems of listening so that he can combat any friction that is disrupting the communication process, this bibliography, which is probably the best one of its kind, is included here.

Enbanks, Ralph T., and others. "A Bibliography of Speech and Theatre in the South for the Year (1954—)." *Southern Speech Journal,* XX (1955—).

Published annually, it covers all areas of speech and drama that are relevant to or published in the thirteen southern states that made up the Confederacy.

Judson, Lyman Spicer. "After Dinner Speaking: A Bibliography," *Quarterly Journal of Speech,* XXIV (1938), 220-27.

Lists both textbooks, speech collections, and important articles dealing with the subject of after-dinner speaking.

Mulgrave, Dorothy, and others. *Bibliography of Speech and Allied Areas, 1950-1960.* New York: Chilton, 1962.

Lists 3,000 doctoral dissertations and books. The allied areas include anatomy, education, fine arts, history, journalism, literature, physiology, and psychology. Subdivisions are given, but there is no index.

Thonssen, Lester, and Fatherson, Elizabeth. *Bibliography of Speech Education.* New York: H. W. Wilson, 1939. Supplement: Thonssen, Robb, and Thonssen. 1950.

Considered to be the most comprehensive bibliographical work in the field, it covers books and articles in all areas of speech and drama.

Collections

Speech collections are invaluable to the student. They may be used to increase his comprehension of the communication process and strategy, as models to guide a beginning speaker through the construction of his own speeches, or they may be used to find speeches quickly in the event that an instructor gives a rhetorical criticism assignment. The following is a list of some of the most useful speech collections.

Representative American Speeches. New York: Wilson, 1938—.

Edited by such men as Albert Craig Baird, Lester Thonssen, and Waldo W. Braden, it appears annually as one number of the

Reference Shelf. Various types of representative speeches of the year from different fields are included, not just political speeches. Some background information concerning the speech and speaker is also usually given.

Brewer, David Josiah, and others. *World's Best Orations; from the Earliest Period to the Present Time.* St. Louis: Kaiser, 1899-1901.

Arranged alphabetically by the speaker's name, it gives a short biographical sketch and selected orations for each entry. Especially valuable for those interested in the historical approach, it indexes orators, subjects, and events and also has chronological indexes of orators, periods and events, law, government, politics, religion and philosophy, literature, and a section called "Noted Sayings & Celebrated Passages."

Prochnow, Herbert Victor. *1400 Ideas for Speakers and Toast-masters: How to Speak with Confidence.* Natick, Mass.: Wilde, 1964.

Collection of humorous stories, epigrams, unusual facts and illustrations, selections from speeches, quotations, and unusual comments, etc. It will help a speaker find appropriate, interesting material that will help get and keep the audience's attention and good will.

Vital Speeches of the Day. New York: City News Publishing Co., 1934-.

Monthly journal that prints important speeches (usually heavily edited) by recognized leaders of public opinion in America. Generally, it covers both sides of public questions, thereby offering the significant thought of leading minds on current national problems. The journal explains that its purpose is to offer students "the finest textbook material . . . from those who have attained leadership in the fields of politics, economics, education, sociology, government, criminology, finance, business, taxation, health, law, labor. . . . "

Currently Published Collections of Speeches

Aly, Bower, and Aly, Lucile F. *American Short Speeches: An Anthology*. New York: Macmillan, 1968.

Baird, A. Craig. *American Public Address*. Hightstown, New Jersey: McGraw-Hill, 1956.

Bolding, Amy. *New Welcome Speeches*. Grand Rapids, Michigan: Baker Books, 1971.

Brandt, Carl G., and Shafter, Edward M., Jr., eds. *Selected American Speeches on Basic Issues (1850-1950)*. Boston: Houghton Mifflin, 1960.

Bryant, D. C. et al. *Historical Anthology of Select British Speeches*. 2nd ed. New York: Ronald, 1967.

Campbell, Karlyn K. *Critiques of Contemporary Rhetoric*. Belmont, Calif.: Wadsworth, 1972.

Capp, Glenn R., ed. *Famous Speeches in American History*. Indianapolis: Bobbs-Merrill, 1963.

Capp, Glenn R. *Great Society: A Sourcebook of Speeches*. Belmont, Calif.: Dickenson, 1967.

Copeland, Lewis, ed. *World's Great Speeches*. 2nd ed. New York: Dover, 1958.

Crystal, David, and Davy, Derek. *Investigating English Style*. Bloomington: Indiana University Press, 1970.

Devlin, L. Patrick. *Contemporary Political Speaking*. Belmont, Calif.: Wadsworth, 1972.

Droke, Maxwell. *The Speaker's Handbook of Humor*. New York: Harper & Row, 1956.

Dunbar, Alice M., ed. *Masterpieces of Negro Eloquence: The Best Speeches Delivered by the Negro from the Days of Slavery to the Present Day*. New York: Johnson Representatives, 1970.

Eavey, C. B. *Ninety-Five Brief Talks for Various Occasions*. Grand Rapids, Michigan: Baker Book House, 1971.

Graham, John. *Great American Speeches, 1898-1963: Texts and Studies*. New York: Appleton, 1970.

Matson, Floyd W., ed. *Voices of Crisis*. New York: Odyssey, 1966.

Speeches in English. New York: Random House, 1968.

Woodson, Carter Godwin, ed. *Negro Orators and Their Orations.* New York: Russell & Russell, 1969.

Dissertations

Dissertations, as sources of both interesting and comprehensive studies, have too long been ignored by students. The following is a list of sources that will guide a student to the dissertations in the field of speech. *Dissertation Abstracts,* another major source of this type of information, is found in the General Reference Works section of this book on page 76.

Auer, John Jeffery. *Doctoral Dissertations in Speech: Work in Progress, 1951-1969.*

Arranged by subject, it is found in volume 18 of *Speech Monographs* and lists dissertations that were in the process of being written. As of 1970, it has been published in the *Bibliographic Annual in Speech Communication,* which is listed on page 123 of this guide.

Dow, Clyde W. *Abstracts of Dissertations in the Field of Speech, 1946-1969.*

Found in *Speech Monographs,* volume 13, from 1946 to 1969, this is an annual listing giving abstracts, or summaries, of doctor's dissertations and master's essays. Many times, enough information will be provided here, so that the student will not have to go the actual dissertation. It is now published in *Bibliographic Annual in Speech Communication,* which is described on page 123.

Knower, Franklin H. *Graduate Theses: An Index of Graduate Work in Speech, 1935-1969.*

Found in *Speech Monographs,* volume 2, the first installment covers 1902-1934. Thereafter it appeared annually, including completed doctor's and master's theses. Now published in the *Bibliographic Annual in Speech Communication,* page 123.

Handbooks, Histories, and Criticism
Baskerville, Barnet. "Selected Writings on the Criticism of Public Address," *Western Speech* (Spring 1957).

An example of what Robert L. Scott and Bernard L. Brock call the experiential perspective.

Black, Edwin. *Rhetorical Criticism: A Study in Method.* New York: Macmillan, 1965.

Listed in *Methods of Rhetorical Criticism: A Twentieth Century Perspective* by Robert L. Scott and Bernard L. Brock as containing examples of what they call the traditional and experiential perspectives.

Brigance, William Norwood, ed. vols. I & II; and Hochmuth (Nichols), Marie Kathryn, ed. vol. III. *A History and Criticism of American Public Address.* New York: Longmans, Green & Co., 1943-1955.

Includes detailed criticisms and style analyses of the most famous American speakers from the Colonial period to World War II. It was prepared under the auspices of the National Association of Teachers of Speech.

Burke, Kenneth. "A Dramatistic View of the Origins of Language," *The Quarterly Journal of Speech;* "Part One," XXXVIII, 3 October 1952, pp. 251-264; "Part Two," XXXVIII, 4 December 1952, pp. 446-460; and "Part Three," XXXIX, 1 February 1953, pp. 79-92.

According to Scott and Brock, all of Burke's works listed here are examples of the "New Rhetorics."

Burke, Kenneth. "Postscripts on the Negative," *The Quarterly Journal of Speech,* XXXIX, 2 April 1953, pp. 209-216.

Burke, Kenneth. *A Rhetoric of Motives.* Englewood Cliffs, N.J.: Prentice-Hall, 1950.

Burke, Kenneth. *The Rhetoric of Religion.* Boston: Beacon Press, 1961.

Clark, Donald Lemen. *Rhetoric in Greco-Roman Education.* New York: Columbia University Press, 1957.

A historical summary of classical rhetoric. Contains a list of "Greek and Roman Primary Sources in Available Editions and Translations."

Fogarty, Daniel. *Roots for a New Rhetoric.* New York: Teachers College Press, 1959.

An example of the "New Rhetoric."

Nichols, Marie Hochmuth. "Kenneth Burke and the 'New Rhetoric,'" *The Quarterly Journal of Speech,* XXXVIII, 2 April 1952, pp. 133-144.

A discussion of the "New Rhetoric" recommended by Scott and Brock in *Methods of Rhetorical Criticism: A Twentieth Century Perspective.*

Prochnow, Herbert Victor. *Speaker's Handbook of Epigrams and Witticisms.* New York: Harper, 1955.

Around 5,000 expressions are arranged by colored main headings. Occasionally the author is mentioned, but the exact citation is not given.

Prochnow, Herbert Victor. *The Toastmaster's Handbook.* New York: Prentice-Hall, 1949.

A manual that discusses the responsibilities and techniques of the toastmaster and gives samples of introductions, quotations, stories, etc.

Robert, Henry M. *Robert's Rules of Order.* Glenview, Ill.: Scott, Foresman, 1951.

Originally written in 1876, this book prescribes the way to organize and conduct meetings, lists the duties of officers, and describes the proper function of motions and amendments. Its style is clear and easy to follow, and it is comprehensive enough to answer most questions on proper meeting procedures.

Thonssen, Lester, Baird, Craig A. and Braden, Waldo W. *Speech Criticism: The Development of Standards for Rhetorical Appraisal,* 2nd ed. New York: Ronald Press, 1970.

It includes extensive bibliographies and discusses in depth the history of rhetoric and the major styles and theories of rhetorical criticism along with their critics.

Wichelns, Herbert. "The Literary Criticism of Oratory," in A. M. Drummond (ed.), *Studies in Rhetoric and Public Speaking in Honor of James A. Winans.* New York: Century, 1925.

An example of the traditional perspective from *Methods of Rhetorical Criticism: A Twentieth Century Perspective* by Robert L. Scott and Bernard L. Brock.

Indexes
Sutton, Roberta Briggs. *Speech Index: An Index to 259 Collections of World Famous Orations and Speeches for Various Occasions.* New York: Scarecrow, 1966.

It now includes all the material from the three previous volumes and incorporates new materials and some older items previously overlooked. As a guide to well-known speeches of famous orators and to types of speeches, it covers the years 1935 to 1965. Arranged alphabetically by subject and speaker's name and indexes collections, speech anthologies, a few books on public speaking, and miscellaneous works. It can be a helpful source of ideas when composing speeches.

Journals and Their Indexes
Journals
The Central States Speech Journal. The Central States Speech Association.

Quarterly publication which contains analyses of speeches and short, scholarly articles representative of all the areas of speech, including a few in the field of theatre arts.

Journal of Communication. Lawrence, Kansas: International Communication Association at the Allan Press, Inc.

Clinically orientated, this magazine is able to provide many detailed studies that could be used to support contentions concerning the communication process. This could be useful to both instructors and students in the field. It is published quarterly.

Philosophy and Rhetoric. Pennsylvania State University: Pennsylvania State University Press.

Quarterly publication concerned with rhetoric as a philosophical comment and encourages exploration of relationships between rhetoric and human activities. Literary works are often discussed in these terms, and book reviews are included. Lengthy, sophisticated articles, meant for advanced undergraduates or graduate students.

Quarterly Journal of Speech. Speech Association of America. Statler Hilton Hotel, 33rd Street and 7th Ave., New York, New York 10001, 1914–.

Recommended primarily for schools of higher education, the articles tend to be lengthy and cover every aspect of speech, theater, and even delve into interpretations of the ideas of contemporary personalities.

Southern Speech Communication Journal. Southern Speech Communication Association, 1935–.

Quarterly publication usually containing short, scholarly articles and book reviews in the several areas of speech and a few in theater arts.

Speech Monographs. Speech Association of America. Statler Hilton Hotel, 33rd St. and 7th Ave., New York, New York 10011, 1934–.

Primarily a vehicle for reports on ongoing research in speech at all levels and in all areas. Even though the title implies otherwise, many scholarly articles outside of speech, such as literature or theater, also appear. Students and scholars will find it particularly useful, since it included until 1970 such bibliographies as "Graduate Theses: An Index to Graduate Work in Speech," and "Abstracts of Dissertations in the Field of Speech," both of which are discussed more fully on p. 128 of this research guide.

The Speech Teacher. Speech Association of America. Statler Hilton Hotel, 33rd St. and 7th Ave., New York, 10001, 1952–.

Directed to the teaching of speech on the levels of elementary and secondary education rather than research in the area, articles tend to be methodical and stick mostly to areas considered to be strictly in the field of speech communication. Includes good reviews of new audio-visual equipment, related articles published in other journals, and book reviews that deal with the teaching of speech.

Today's Speech. Speech Association of Eastern States. Dept. of Speech, Rm. 354, Sparks Building, Pennsylvania State University, University Park, Pennsylvania 16802, 1953–.

Emanating from a professional organization, this deals with all phases of speech such as public speaking, drama, therapy, semantics, business and professional communication, and classroom approaches. The editor encourages controversy by including articles and letters on contemporary usage, the communication process, and teaching methods. This helps make the magazine more lively than the *Speech Teacher* or the *Quarterly Journal of Speech.* Both students and teachers benefit from reading it.

Western Speech. Western Speech Communication Association. Dept. of Speech, University of Oregon, Eugene, Oregon 97403, 1936–.

Quarterly publication that consists of scholarly articles dealing with the various areas of speech. There is some attempt to deal with rhetorical principles in some literary works.

Indexes

Gray, Giles Wilkeson (comp.). *Index to the Quarterly Journal of Speech, Volumes I to XL, 1915-1954.* Dubuque, Iowa: (Wm. C. Brown Co.) The Speech Association of America, 1956.

Gray, Giles Wilkeson (comp.). "An Index to *Speech Monographs,* Volumes I-XXVI (1934-1959)," *SM,* XXVII (1960): 155-200.

Knower, Franklin H. (Comp.). *Table of Contents of The Quarterly Journal of Speech, 1915-1960, Speech Monographs, 1934-1960, and The Speech Teacher, 1952-1960.* (Bloomington, Indiana): Speech Association of America, 1961.

Dunham, Robert E., and L. S. Harms. *Index and Table of Contents of Southern Speech Journal, 1937-1960; Western Speech Journal, 1937-1960; Central States Speech Journal, 1949-1960; and Today's Speech, 1953-1960.*
    These may be obtained from the secretaries of the Central States Speech Association, Speech Association of the Eastern States, and Southern Speech Association.

Cartier, Francis A. *Ten-Year Index: Volumes 1-10 (Journal of Communication). Journal of Communication,* 1961. Supplement.

Recent Textbooks in the Field of Speech
(Not necessarily recommended texts)

Fundamentals Texts
Bormann, Ernest G., and Bormann, Nancy C. *Speech Communication: An Interpersonal Approach. New York: Harper & Row, 1972.*

Bosmajian, Haig A. *Readings in Speech.* 2nd ed. New York: Harper & Row, 1971.

Jeffrey, Robert C., and Peterson, Owen. *Speech: A Text with Adapted Readings.* New York: Harper & Row, 1971.

Jensen, J. Vernon. *Perspectives on Oral Communication.* Boston: Holbrook Press, 1970.

McCabe, Bernard P., Jr. *Communicative Voice and Articulation.* Boston: Holbrook Press, 1970.

Oliver, Robert T. *Making Your Meaning Effective.* Boston: Holbrook Press, 1971.

Scott, Robert L., and Brockriede, Wayne. *The Rhetoric of Black Power.* New York: Harper & Row, 1969.

Stedman, William. *A Guide to Public Speaking.* Englewood Cliffs, N.J.: Prentice-Hall, 1971.

Verderber, Rudolph F. *The Challenge of Effective Speaking.* Belmont, Calif.: Wadsworth, 1970.

Language and Phonetics
McNeill, David. *The Acquisition of Language: The Study of Developmental Psycholinguistics.* New York: Harper & Row, 1970.

Voice and Diction
Capp, Glen R. *Basic Oral Communication.* (Revision of *How to Communicate Orally*). 2nd ed. Englewood Cliffs, N.J.: Prentice-Hall, 1971.

Hanley, Theodore D., and Thurman, Wayne L. *Developing Vocal Skills.* Corte Madera, Cal., Rinehart, 1970.

Jones, Merritt, and Pettas, Mary. *Speech Improvement: A Practical Program.* Belmont, Cal.: Wadsworth, 1969.

Rizzo, Raymond. *The Voice As an Instrument.* Indianapolis: The Odyssey Press (Bobbs-Merrill), 1969.

Public Speaking Texts
Barker, Larry L. *Listening Behavior.* Englewood Cliffs, N.J.: Prentice-Hall, 1971.

Howell, William S., and Bormann, Ernest G. *Presentational Speaking for Business and the Professions.* New York: Harper & Row, 1971.

Linkugel, Wil A., and Berg, David M. *A Time to Speak.* Belmont, Calif.: Wadsworth, 1970.

Miller, Arthur B. *Modes of Public Speaking.* Belmont, Calif.: Wadsworth, 1971.

Discussion, Debate, and Parliamentary Procedure Texts
Andersen, Kenneth E. *Persuasion: Theory and Practice.* Boston: Allyn & Bacon, 1971.

Bormann, Ernest G. *Discussion and Group Methods.* New York: Harper & Row, 1969.

Bosmajian, Haig. *The Principles and Practice of Freedom of Speech.* Boston: Houghton Mifflin, 1971.

Freeley, Austin J. *Argumentation and Debate: Rational Decision Making, Third Edition.* Belmont, Cal.: Wadsworth, 1971.

McCroskey, James G. *An Introduction to Rhetorical Communication: The Theory and Practice of Public Speaking.* 2nd ed. Englewood Cliffs, N.J.: Prentice-Hall, 1971.

Thompson, Wayne N. *Modern Argumentation and Debate: Principles and Practices.* New York: Harper & Row, 1971.

Public Address History and Criticism

Bormann, Ernest G. *Forerunners of Black Power: the Rhetoric of Abolition.* Englewood Cliffs, N.J.: Prentice-Hall, 1971.

Brandes, Paul D. *The Rhetoric of Revolt.* Englewood Cliffs, N.J.: Prentice-Hall, 1971.

Smith, Arthur L., and Robb, Stephen, eds. *The Voice of Black Rhetoric.* Boston: Allyn & Bacon, 1971.

Weiss, Robert O., and Brock, Bernard L., eds. *Current Criticism: Essays from Speaker and Gavel.* Slippery Rock, Pennsylvania: Delta Sigma Rho-Tau Kappa Alpha, 1971.

Communication

Barker, Larry L., and Kibler, Robert J., eds. *Speech Communication Behavior: Perspectives and Principles.* Englewood Cliffs, N.J.: Prentice-Hall, 1971.

Bem, Daryl J. *Beliefs, Attitudes, and Human Affairs.* Belmont, Calif.: Brooks/Cole (Wadsworth), 1970.

Campbell, James H., and Hepler, Hal W. *Dimensions in Communication: Readings, Second Edition.* Belmont, Calif.: Wadsworth, 1970.

DeFleur, Melvin L. *Theories of Mass Communication.* New York: McKay, 1970.

DeVito, Joseph. *Communication: Concepts and Processes.* Englewood Cliffs, N.J.: Prentice-Hall, 1971.

Egan, Gerard. *Encounter: Group Processes for Interpersonal Growth.* Belmont, Calif.: Brooks/Cole (Wadsworth), 1970.

Eisenberg, Abne M. and Smith, Ralph R. *Non-Verbal Communication.* Indianapolis: Bobbs-Merrill, 1972.

Emmert, Philip, and Brooks, William D. *Methods of Research in Communication.* Boston: Houghton Mifflin, 1970.

Garvin, Paul L. *Cognition: A Multiple View.* New York: Spartan Books, 1971.

Giffin, Kim, and Patton, Bobby R. *Basic Readings in Interpersonal Communication.* New York: Harper & Row, 1971.

Giffin, Kim, and Patton, Bobby R. *Fundamentals of Interpersonal Communication.* New York: Harper & Row, 1971.

Keltner, John W. *Interpersonal Speech-Communication.* Belmont, Calif.: Wadsworth, 1970.

McCroskey, James C., Larson, Carl L., and Knapp, Mark L. *An Introduction to Interpersonal Communication.* Englewood Cliffs, N.J.: Prentice-Hall, 1971.

Mehrabian, Albert. *Silent Messages.* Belmont, Calif.: Wadsworth, 1972.

Ross,, Raymond S. *Speech Communication: Fundamentals and Practice.* 2nd ed. Englewood Cliffs, N.J.: Prentice-Hall, 1970.

Scheflin, Albert E. *Stream and Structure in Communicational Behavior.* Bloomington: Indiana University Press, 1971.

Schmidt, Warren H. *Organizational Frontiers and Human Values.* Belmont, Calif.: Wadsworth, 1970.

Sereno, Kenneth K., and Mortensen, C. David. *Foundations of Communication Theory.* New York: Harper & Row, 1970.

Smith, Raymond G. *Speech Communication: Theory and Models.* New York: Harper & Row, 1970.

Thayer, Lee. *Communication: General Semantics Perspectives.* New York: Spartan Books, 1970.

Interpretation Texts

Brooks, Keith; Bahn, Eudgen; and Okey, L. Lamont. *Literature for Listening: An Oral Interpreter's Anthology.* Boston: Allyn & Bacon, 1968.

Lee, Charlotte I. *Oral Interpretation.* 4th ed. Boston: Houghton Mifflin, 1971.

Mattingly, Alethea Smith, and Grimes, Wilma H. *Interpretation: Writer-Reader-Audience.* 2nd Ed. Belmont, Calif.: Wadsworth, 1970.

Fitzgerald, Burdette S. *World Tales for Creative Dramatics and Storytelling.* Englewood Cliffs, N.J.: Prentice-Hall, 1962.

RADIO, TELEVISION, AND FILM

General Texts

Head, Sydney W. *Broadcasting in America: A Survey of Television and Radio.* 2nd ed. Boston: Houghton Mifflin, 1971.

Hyde, Stuart W. *Television and Radio Announcing.* 2nd ed. Boston: Houghton Mifflin, 1971.

Rivers, William L.; Paterson, Theodore; and Jensen, Jay W. *The Mass Media and Modern Society.* Corte Madera, Cal.: Rinehart, 1971.

Radio Texts

Jones, Kenneth E., and Johnson, Joseph S. *Modern Radio Station Practices.* Belmont, Calif.: Wadsworth, 1972.

Kirschner, Allen, and Kirschner, Linda. *Readings in the Mass Media: Radio & Television.* Indianapolis: The Odyssey Press (Bobbs-Merrill), 1971.

Television Texts

Green, Maury. *Television News: Anatomy and Process.* Belmont, Calif.: Wadsworth, 1969.

Zettl, Herbert. *Television Production Workbook, Second Edition.* Belmont, Calif.: Wadsworth, 1968.

Zettl, Herbert. *Television Production Handbook, Second Edition.* Belmont, Calif.: Wadsworth, 1968.

Speech Education

Egland, George O. *Speech and Language Problems: A Guide for the Classroom Teacher.* Englewood Cliffs, N.J.: Prentice-Hall, 1970.

Nelson, Oliver W., and LaRusso, Dominic A. *Oral Communication in the Secondary School Classroom.* Englewood Cliffs, N.J.: Prentice-Hall, 1970.

Phillips, Gerald M.; Dunham, Robert; Brubaker, Robert; and Butt, David. *The Development of Oral Communication in the Classroom.* Indianapolis: Bobbs-Merrill, 1970.

Brooks, W. D., and Friedrich, Gustav W. *Teaching Speech Com-*

munication in the Secondary Schools. Boston: Houghton Mifflin, 1972.

Specialized Areas

DISCUSSION AND DEBATE

Bibliography

Kruger, Arthur N. *A Classified Bibliography of Argumentation and Debate.* New York: Scarecrow, 1964.

Covering all phases of debating, this comprehensive bibliography of books and articles in English, primarily from the 20th century, also includes master's and doctor's theses.

Indexes

Debate Index. Joseph R. Dunlap, and Martin A. Kuhn (comp.). 2nd Supplement. New York: Wilson, 1939.

Subject index is a guide to bibliographies, collections of articles on public questions, briefs, and debates.

Handbooks

Auer, John Jeffery, and Ewbank, Henry Lee. *Handbook for Discussion Leaders.* Rev. ed. New York: Harper, 1954.

Handbook that includes information on organizing, conducting, and evaluating group discussions, panels, symposiums, lectures, debates, and forums.

Baird, Albert Craig. *Argumentation, Discussion, and Debate.* New York: McGraw-Hill, 1950.

Ewbank, Henry Lee, and Auer, John Jeffery. *Discussion and Debate; Tools of a Democracy.* 2nd ed. New York: Appleton, 1951.

Hare, Paul A. *Handbook of Small Group Research.* New York: Free Press of Glencoe, 1962.

Considered one of the most complete reference works in its area. Of the nearly 1400 studies completed between 1900 and 1959, many are summarized.

Reference Shelf. New York: H. W. Wilson, 1922—.

Each of the six numbers to each volume covers a timely controversial question. Reprints of selected articles from books and periodicals give background information and pro and con arguments. A comprehensive bibliography is included.

Walch, John Weston. *Complete Handbook On . . . .* Portland, Me.: J. Weston Walch, 1936—.

Issued annually in two series: (1) on the topic for the collegiate debate of the year; (2) on the topic of the high school debate of the year. Gives background information; arguments pro and con; statistics, facts, and opinions on the subject; quotations with exact citations to sources; and annotated bibliographies.

LOGIC
Beach, John D. *Introduction to Logic.* Boston: Allyn & Bacon, 1970.

Brennan, Joseph Gerard. *A Handbook of Logic.* New York: Harper, 1957.

Martin, Richard Milton. *Logic, Language and Metaphysics.* New York: New York University Press, 1971.

Resnik, Michael D. *Elementary Logic.* New York: McGraw-Hill, 1970.

MASS MEDIA—RADIO AND TELEVISION AND AUDIO-VISUAL COMMUNICATION
General Guides and Bibliographies

Adkins, Gale R. *Books on Radio-Television-Film; A Collection of Recommendations.* Lawrence: The University of Kansas, Radio-Television Research, 1962.

Lists 348 books that have been recommended by teachers of broadcasting and film. It includes books, some annotated, on history, social influence, regulations, script collections, etc.

"Articles on Mass Communications in Magazines of the U.S.A.: A Selected Annotated Bibliography," *Journalism Quarterly,* VII (1930–).

Appearing quarterly, it is a selective bibliography from trade, popular, and scholarly periodicals. Aspects of production are not covered.

Blum, Eleanor. *Reference Books in the Mass Media: An Annotated, Selected Booklist Covering Book Publishing, Broadcasting, Films, Newspapers, Magazines, and Advertising.* Urbana: University of Illinois Press, 1962.

Compiled for students and laymen in mass communications, it provides facts, names and addresses and suggestions for beginning research. Annotated listed sources are arranged under six major subject headings: General and background books, book publishing, broadcasting, films, newspapers and magazines, and advertising and public relations.

Bogart, Leo. *The Age of Television; A Study of Viewing Habits and the Impact of Television on American Life.* 2nd ed., rev. and enlarged. New York: Ungar, 1958.

Summarizes the published research on television audiences and emphasizes survey research. A bibliography is included.

Current Mass Communication Research—I. Paris: UNESCO, 1957.

Includes a bibliography of the area of books and articles published in 1955-56. It is a register of research projects in progress from twenty-four different countries.

Klapper, Joseph T. *The Effects of Mass Communication.* Glencoe, Ill.: Free Press, 1960.

Some of the most important research in the area is brought together and compared here. A bibliography is included.

Reference Books for Broadcasters. Washington, D.C.: National Association of Broadcasters, 1962.

Compiled for professional broadcasters, but is widely used, it is an excellent guide to reference books in the field.

Saunders, James G. (comp.). "Analysis of Broadcast Literature: Periodical Publications in Psychology, 1950-1960, an Annotated Bibliography," *Journal of Broadcasting,* VI (1961-62): 75-91.

Lists research done in the fields of advertising, audience behavior and media effects, instructional broadcasting, production and programming, and research methodology.

Television, Cinema and Radio Advertising Directory 1969-70. 2nd ed. London: Admark Directories; distr. International Publications Service, 1969.

Includes an international directory by country of television and radio stations, production companies, advertisers and agents, and a directory of studio and theater services, directors, producers, script writers, etc.

Communication Facilities and Organizations
Basic Facts and Figures; International Statistics Relating to Education, Culture and Mass Communication. Paris: UNESCO, 1952—. Irregular.

Includes data and figures on film production, population, movie houses, and radio and television receivers in approximately 200 countries.

Chapin, Richard E. *Mass Communications; A Statistical Analysis.* East Lansing, Mich.: Michigan State University Press, 1957.

Source for statistics and recent data in the area of the mass media.

Paterson, Wilbur C. *Organizations, Publications and Directories in the Mass Media of Communications.* Iowa City: State University of Iowa, School of Journalism, 1960.

Lists and describes nearly 250 organizations, directories, and publications in the field.

Press, Film, and Radio; Reports of the Commission on Technical Needs. 5 vols. Paris: UNESCO, 1947-51. 2 suppls.

Includes information on education and facilities for media personnel in many different countries.

World Communications: Press, Radio, Film, Television. Paris: UNESCO, 1956.

Communication facilities of different countries are reported including information such as the following: ownership and regulation of stations, number of radio and television stations and receivers, and number of films produced each year.

Broadcasting

BBC Handbook. London: British Broadcasting Corporation, 1928–.

Includes information on the yearly operation of the B.B.C., an index, and a current bibliography on British broadcasting. For 1930-34 and 1943-52 it was called *B.B.C. Year-book*; in 1935-37 it was called *B.B.C. Annual*; not published in 1953-54.

British Broadcasting: A Bibliography. London: British Broadcasting Corporation, 1958. Supplement, 1958-60. (1961).

Includes books on broadcasting, except for those on engineering subjects, published in Great Britain; a list of articles on B.B.C. policy; and important Parliament debates and official publications relating to the B.B.C. A section in each issue of the *B.B.C. Handbook* keeps it current.

Broadcasting-Telecasting Yearbook. Washington, D.C.: Broadcasting Publications, Inc., 1931–. Title varies.

Published annually, it gives information on key broadcasting personnel in the United States, station rates, codes, advertising agencies, the stations, and the networks, etc.

Cooper, Isabella M. *Bibliography on Educational Broadcasting.* Chicago: University of Chicago Press, 1942.

Includes problems of censorship, news, propaganda, as well as the other areas that are normally thought of as being "educational." Annotated.

Fielding, Raymond. "Broadcast Literature in Motion Picture Periodicals: A Bibliography," *Journal of Broadcasting,* III (1959): 172-92.

Emphasizes the aspects of broadcasting that are of prime concern to the motion picture industry.

Hamill, Patricia B., and Broderick, Gertrude G. *Radio and Television, A Selective Bibliography.* Bulletin 1960, no. 25. Washington, D.C.: Office of Education, 1960.

Particularly good because it includes a list of script collections.

Harwood, Kenneth. "A World Bibliography of Selected Periodicals on Broadcasting," *Journal of Broadcasting,* V (1961): 251-78.

Designed to show the variety of periodical literature available in broadcasting. Usually the name and address of publishers are included. The arrangement is geographical.

Heath, Harry, and Wolfson, Joel. "Analysis of Broadcast Literature: Broadcast Journalism in 'Education on the Air': 1930-1953," *Journal of Broadcasting,* VI (1962): 363-68.

Bibliography indexing news-related materials in *Education on the Air,* the magazine for the Institute for Education by Radio-Television. Annual volumes provide information concerning the development of educational broadcasting in the United States.

Kahn, Frank J., ed. *Documents of American Broadcasting.* New York: Appleton, 1969.

Well edited collection of primary sources including laws, important decisions and other documents illustrating the history of broadcasting as well as a bibliography.

McKune, Lawrence E. (comp.). *Telecourses for Credit.* East Lansing, Mich.: Michigan State University, Continuing Education Service, 1954—.

Main subject is courses offered for credit on television in the United States. Details such as the sponsoring school, number of credits, enrollment, fees, and course administration are included.

Pike and Fischer Radio Regulation. 24 vols. Washington, D.C.: Pike and Fischer, Inc., 1948—.

Most complete and current source of information on the regulations of television and radio, it contains information on FCC decisions and reports, statutes, forms, court cases and standards. It is kept up-to-date with loose-leaf supplements.

Rose, Oscar. *Radio Broadcasting and Television; An Annotated Bibliography.* New York: H. W. Wilson, 1947.

Covers nontechnical books and pamphlets published in the United States up to 1946.

United Nations Educational, Scientific and Cultural Organization. *World Radio and Television.* Paris: UNESCO, 1965.

Describes the existing television and radio facilities in nearly 200 countries, material being drawn from UNESCO's *World Communications.* A bibliography is included.

Journals

Broadcasting. Sol Taishoff. 1735 DeSales St., N.W. Washington, D.C.: Broadcasting Publications. Inc., 1931—.

Designed for professionals in the radio and television field, it is aimed at advertising agencies, networks, stations, program suppliers, and equipment manufacturers among others. It reports Federal Communication Commission's regulations, legislation concerning broadcasting, and legal procedures and covers latest trends, statistics and developments in the field of communication. It is an important magazine for those taking radio or television courses. The *Broadcasting Yearbook* includes much valuable information concerning business, economic, and technical facts relating to broadcasting and associated arts and services.

Journal of Broadcasting. Association for Professional Broadcasting Education. Temple University, Philadelphia, Penn. 19122, 1956–.

Quarterly publication containing scholarly and helpful articles in the area of reporting and television or radio broadcasting and also book reviews in areas of mass media. It occasionally gives valuable bibliographies—i.e. spring 1972 included a *World Bibliography of Selected Periodicals on Broadcasting.*

NAEB Journal. National Assn. of Educational Broadcasters. Gregory Hall, University of Illinois, Urbana, Ill. 61801, 1941–.

One objective source of news and developments in educational television and radio, it provides information on government financing and other activities and articles for the teacher using and directing educational television programs. However, this is important information for any school or person wishing to be informed on major developments in this important educational field.

Audio-Visual Communication
Allen, William H. *Audio-Visual Communication Research.* Santa Monica, Calif.: Systems Development Corp., 1958.

Reviews the major research done in the area of audio-visual communication and includes an extensive bibliography.

Educational Media Index. New York: McGraw-Hill, 1964.

Although it has many inadequacies, it is an attempt to provide information as to the source, content, and cost of non-book material in the audio-visual and visual materials field, including charts, maps, programmed material, models, etc. The thirteen volumes and master index indicate the subject areas and the appropriate educational level of the material available. This index helped begin the National Information Center for Educational Media located at the University of Southern California. It supersedes and extends the *Educational Film Guide.* New York: H. H. Wilson, 1936-61. Annual.

Filmstrips on Current Affairs. New York: New York Times, 1971-72.

Only guide to printed and audio-visual material on current topics of national and international importance. Useful for high school, college, and adult audiences and includes a complete study guide with each topic.

Hartman, Frank R. "Single and Multiple Channel Communication: A Review of Research and a Proposed Model," *Audio-Visual Communication Review,* VI (1961): 235-62.

Bibliography on studies of effectiveness of different channels of communication.

Larson, Lawrence C., and Runden, C. E., (eds.). *Bibliography of Research in Audio-Visual Education and Mass Media, 1930-1950.* Bloomington, Ind.: Indiana University, Audio-Visual Center, 1950.

McClusky, Frederick D. *A-V Bibliography.* 2nd ed. Dubuque, Iowa: Wm. C. Brown, 1955.

Has an annotated bibliography on research in audio-visual communication and lists doctoral dissertations in the field from 1921-54.

National Information Center for Educational Media. New York: Bowker, 1969.

Supplants the older *Educational Media Index.* See p. 146.

"Research Abstracts and Analytical Review of Completed Projects: National Defense Education Act, Title VII," *Audio-Visual Communication Review,* IX (1961–).

Published irregularly, it contains summaries and reviews of research on learning through the various areas of the mass media.

Rufsvold, Irene Margaret, and Guss, Carolyn. *Guides to Newer Educational Media.* 2nd ed. Chicago: American Library Association, 1967.

Especially good for beginners in the area, it includes annotated catalogs, lists, and periodicals that provide the most up-to-date information on the new types of educational media. The book lists such equipment as 16mm motion pictures; 35mm filmstrips; 2″ X 2″ and 3¼″ X 4″ slides; kinescopes and videotapes; phonodiscs and phonotapes; transparencies; and programmed instruction materials. Be sure to read the Preface carefully in order to use the guide effectively.

Thomas, Gordon L., and Potter, David. "A 'Discography' of Commercially Recorded Speeches," *The Speech Teacher,* VI (1957): 18-26.

Magazines on Audio-Visual Communication
Audiovisual Instruction. National Education Assn., Dept. of Audio-visual Instruction, 1201 16th St., N.W., Washington, D.C. 20036, 1956—.

Includes articles giving practical information about audio-visual equipment and techniques. A section called "News Notes" reviews records, films, and new equipment in the field. It even indexes audio-visual reviews from other publications. Issued from September to June.

Educator's Guide to Media and Methods. Media and Methods Institute, Inc., 134 N. 13th St., Philadelphia, Pa. 19107, 1964—.

Probably the best general audio-visual magazine available. Included are many how-to articles concerning creative and effective methods and media in the high school classroom and articles on media theory. A must for schools of education, and valuable to speakers wishing to communicate as fully and as dramatically as possible. Issued from September to May.

ORAL INTERPRETATION OF LITERATURE
Grimes, Wilma H. "Oral Interpretation and Criticism: A Bibliography," *Western Speech,* XXII (1958): 69-74.

Good resource for teachers, researchers, and speakers.

PSYCHOLOGY

Bird, Charles. "Suggestion and Suggestibility: Bibliography," *Psychological Bulletin,* XXXVI (1939): 264-83.

Indexed by subject, methodology, and variables, this source is especially strong in the area of persuasion.

Hunt, William A. "Recent Developments in the Field of Emotion," *Psychological Bulletin,* XXXVIII (1941): 249-76.

Reviews all types of research, but emphasizes laboratory experimentation.

Krasner, Leonard. "Studies of the Conditioning of Verbal Behavior," *Psychological Bulletin,* LV (1958): 148-70.

Summarizes experiments on verbal behavior and has a comprehensive bibliography.

Salzinger, Kurt. "Experimental Manipulation of Verbal Behavior: A Review," *Journal of General Psychology,* LXI (1959): 65-94.

Has a good bibliography.

Sanford, Fillmore H. "Speech and Personality," *Psychological Bulletin,* XXXIX (1942): 811-45.

Reviews research in the area and has a bibliography.

Vallance, T. R. "Methodology in Propaganda Research," *Psychological Bulletin, XLVIII (1951): 32-61.*

Reviews research and theory in the field.

Books

Brown, R. *Social Psychology.* New York: Free Press, 1965.

Evans, R. I., & Rozelle, R. M. *Social Psychology in Life.* Boston: Allyn & Bacon, 1970.

Freedman, J. L.; Carlsmith, J. M.; & Sears, D. O. *Social Psychology.* Englewood Cliffs, N.J.: Prentice-Hall, 1970.

Hall, C. S., & Lindzey, G. *Theories of Personality.* (2nd ed.) New York: Wiley, 1970.

Hovland, Carl Iver, et al. *The Order of Presentation in Persuasion.* Vol. 1, Yale Study in Attitude and Communication. New Haven, Conn.: Yale University Press, 1966.

Insko, C. A., & Schopler, J. *Experimental Social Psychology.* New York: Academic Press, 1972.

Jones, E. E., & Gerard, H. B. *Foundations of Social Psychology.* New York: Wiley, 1967.

Maddi, S. R. *Personality Theories: A Comparative Analysis.* Homewood, Ill.: Dorsey Press, 1968.

Mischel, W. *Introduction to Personality.* New York: Holt, Rinehart & Winston, 1971.

Sarason, I. G. *Personality: An Objective Approach.* New York: Wiley, 1966.

Part III

ADDITIONAL INFORMATION
FOR THE STUDENT
OF SPEECH

Rules and Techniques
of Successful Interviewing

The interview as a research technique is increasing and probably will continue to do so. The following rules will help achieve a smooth and successful interview. The following techniques are paraphrased from American University's Washington Semester Program.

1. Try to make an appointment. Do not just "drop in" on a busy official unless he has invited you to do so, or unless you have been unable to get his office to give you an appointment.
2. Be prompt for appointments. Leave a sufficient safety margin in your travel time to the appointment to cover accidental delays and getting lost.
3. While waiting to be shown in, verify the spelling of the name and title of the official you are going to interview, and the pronunciation of his name, if in doubt. Write these things down for your bibliography and other later uses. Mark down the date of the interview.
4. Ask the secretary for printed materials that might be available.
5. Begin the interview by telling who you are, why you are doing the project, and what it is about.
6. Have several specific questions prepared, covering your purpose for being there. These should be ones that fill necessary gaps remaining in your information after you have done all the reading for the project.

These questions may then lead to others.

7. Take notes or use a tape recorder only with permission, and even then, only if you are sure that doing so will not destroy the usefulness of the interview. Sometimes it is better to wait until the interview is over to note what was said.

8. Do not quote one official to another!

9. Remember that bodily movements and facial expressions—especially eye contact—communicate your attitude to the person being interviewed.

10. Thank the person interviewed and leave just as soon as you feel that you have the information you need, unless he is clearly not busy and is willing to talk further. Do not overstay your welcome.

11. Write a note of thanks to the person interviewed within a week. This should be regarded as a strict obligation. No single act does more for the benefit of future students seeking similar interviews.

Remember that you are carrying the reputation of your high school or college on your shoulders when interviewing. If you leave behind you a trail of irritation, or have presented yourself ill-prepared, or failed to show courtesy and gratitude, you will make life that much harder for other students who may come later to interview the same people.

As a final note about interviewing, bear in mind that you are doing serious research. The number of interviews is far less important than the quality of the information gained. Seek out the knowledgeable, not the garrulous, and, when appropriate, ask each interviewee for suggestions for other interviews.

Correspondence with Government Officials

WRITING TIPS

Rep. Morris K. Udall (Dem., Ariz.) and the League of Women Voters have provided these hints on how to write to a member of Congress:

Write to your own Senator or Congressman. Letters sent to others will end up on the desk of your representative eventually anyway.

Write at the proper time, when a bill is being discussed in committee or on the floor.

Use your own words and your own stationery. Avoid signing and sending a form or mimeographed letter.

Do not be a pen pal. Don't try to instruct the Representative or Senator on every issue that comes up.

Do not demand a commitment before all the facts are in. Bills rarely become law in the same form as they are introduced.

Identify all bills by their title or their number.

If possible, include pertinent editorials from local papers.

Be constructive. If a bill deals with a problem you admit exists, but you believe the bill is the wrong approach, tell what you think the right approach is.

If you have expert knowledge or wide experience in a particular area, share it with the appropriate person. But do not pretend to wield vast political influence.

Write to a member of Congress when he does something you approve of. A note of appreciation will make him remember you more favorably the next time.

Feel free to write when you have a question or problem dealing with procedures of government departments.

Be brief, write legibly, and be sure to use the proper form of address.

Correct Form for Writing to Government Officials

President

The President
The White House
Washington, D.C. 20500

Dear Mr. President:
Very respectfully yours,

Vice-President

The Vice President
The White House
Washington, D.C. 20500

Dear Mr. Vice President:
Sincerely yours,

Senator

The Honorable [Full Name]
United States Senate
Washington, D.C. 20510

Dear Senator [Name]:
Sincerely yours,

Representative

The Honorable [Full Name]
House of Representatives
Washington, D.C. 20515

Dear Mr. [Name]:
Sincerely yours,

Member of the Cabinet

The Honorable [Full Name]
The Secretary of the Treasury
Washington, D.C. 20520

Dear Mr. Secretary:
Sincerely yours,

Informational Services in the United States

National and International Interest Groups

There are countless interest groups with offices in Washington, D.C. that can provide information on their particular concerns. Often a simple postcard is all that is necessary to request information. A more complete listing can be found in *The Encyclopedia of Associations* (Detroit: Gale Research Co., 1968).

African-American Institute
Room 500,
1346 Connecticut Avenue, NW
Washington, D.C.

Air Traffic Control Association
Room 409,
525 School Street, SW
Washington, D.C.

American Association for the Advancement of Science
1515 Massachusetts Avenue
Washington, D.C.

American Association of Junior Colleges
Project Focus 1155 15th Street, NW
Washington, D.C.

American Council on Education
1 Dupont Circle, NW
Washington, D.C.

American Farm Bureau Federation
425 Thirteenth Street, NW
Washington, D.C.

American Federation of Labor and Congress of Industrial Organizations
815 Sixteenth Street, NW
Washington, D.C.

American Friends of the Middle East
1717 Massachusetts Avenue
Washington, D.C.

American Institute of Architects
1785 Massachusetts Avenue, NW
Washington, D.C.

American Israel Public Affairs Committee
Colo Building
Washington, D.C.

American Legion
1608 K Street, NW
Washington, D.C.

American Peace Society
4000 Albemarle Street, NW
Washington, D.C.

American Petroleum Institute
1801 K Street, NW
Washington, D.C.

American Public Power Association
2600 Virginia Avenue
Washington, D.C.

Americans for Constitutional Action
955 L'Enfant Plaza N., SW
Washington, D.C.

Americans for Democratic Action
1424 Sixteenth Street, NW
Washington, D.C.

*Anti-Communist World Freedom
    Congress, Inc.*
8801 MacArthur Boulevard, NW
Washington, D.C.

American Veterans Committee
1333 Connecticut Avenue, NW
Washington, D.C.

Chamber of Commerce of the U.S.
1129 20th Street, NW
Washington, D.C.

*Chiefs of Police, International
    Association of Police Chiefs*
11 Firstfield Road
Washington, D.C.

Civil Liberties Union
1424 Sixteenth Street, NW
Washington, D.C.

*Council of Graduate Schools of
    the U.S.*
1 Dupont Circle
Washington, D.C.

Council of State Governments
1735 DeSales Street, NW
Washington, D.C.

Defense Supply Association
1026 Seventeenth Street, NW
Washington, D.C.

Distilled Spirits Institute
425 Thirteenth Street, NW
Washington, D.C.

Fair Campaign Practices Committee
328 Pennsylvania Avenue, SE
Washington, D.C.

Society of American Foresters
1010 Sixteenth Street, NW
Washington, D.C.

Home Study Council, National
1601 Eighteenth Street, NW
Washington, D.C.

*League of Women Voters of the
    United States*
1200 Seventeenth Street, NW
Washington, D.C.

*National Association for the
    Advancement of Colored People*
422 First Street, SE
Washington, D.C.

*National Association of Daughters
    of the American Revolution*
1776 D Street, NW
Washington, D.C.

*National Association of Social
    Workers*
1424 Sixteenth Street, NW
Washington, D.C.

*National Committee against Mental
    Illness*
1101 Seventeenth Street, NW
Washington, D.C.

*National Confederation of
    American Ethnic Groups*
1629 K Street, NW
Washington, D.C.

National Council of Negro Women
1346 Connecticut Avenue, NW
Washington, D.C.

National Democratic Committee
2600 Virginia Avenue, NW
Washington, D.C.

National Farmers Union
1012 Fourteenth Street, NW
Washington, D.C.

National Grange
1616 H Street, NW
Washington, D.C.

*National Guard Association
    of the U.S.*
One Massachusetts Avenue, NW
Washington, D.C.

*National Rifle Association
    of America*
1600 Rhode Island Avenue, NW
Washington, D.C.

*National Rivers and Harbors
    Congress*
1028 Connecticut Avenue, NW
Washington, D.C.

National Sheriffs' Association
1250 Connecticut Avenue, NW
Washington, D.C.

Navy League of the U.S.
818 Eighteenth Street, NW
Washington, D.C.

Peanut Council, National
1120 Connecticut Avenue, NW
Washington, D.C.

Pharmaceutical Manufacturers
1155 Fifteenth Street, NW
Washington, D.C.

Right-to-Work Committee
1900 L Street, NW
Washington, D.C.

*Student Nonviolent Coordinating
    Committee*
2208 Fourteenth Street, NW
Washington, D.C.

Taxpayers Association, American
501 Thirteenth Street, NW
Washington, D.C.

The Urban Coalition
2100 M Street, NW
Washington, D.C.

*United Nations Association of the
    USA*
2501 Calvert, NW
Washington, D.C.

*United States Army, Association
    of the*
1529 Eighteenth Street, NW
Washington, D.C.

United World Federalists
2029 K Street, NW
Washington, D.C.

*Young Democratic Clubs of
    America*
2600 Virginia Avenue, NW
Washington, D.C.

*Young Republican National
    Federation*
310 First Street, SE
Washington, D.C.

World Wildlife Fund
910 Seventeenth Street, NW
Washington, D.C.

The United Nations

INFORMATION SERVICES IN THE UNITED STATES OF MEMBERS OF THE UNITED NATIONS

Like interest groups, nations are usually eager to provide information on their governments and policies. Therefore the following information services are provided.

Afghanistan
Embassy of Afghanistan
2341 Wyoming Avenue, NW
Washington, D.C.

Albania
Permanent Mission of the
    People's Republic of Albania
    to the UN
250 East Eighty-sixth Street
New York, N.Y.

Algeria
Permanent Mission of Algeria
    to the UN
750 Third Avenue
New York, N.Y.

Argentina
Embassy of the Argentine Republic
1600 New Hampshire Avenue, NW
Washington, D.C.

Australia
Australian News and Information
    Bureau
636 Fifth Avenue
New York, N.Y.

Austria
Austrian Information Service
31 East Sixty-ninth Street
New York, N.Y.

Barbados
Barbados Tourist and Development
    Board
801 Second Avenue
New York, N.Y.

Belgium
Belgian Consulate General
50 Rockefeller Plaza
New York, N.Y.

Bolivia
Embassy of Bolivia
1145 Nineteenth Street, NW
Washington, D.C.

Botswana
Permanent Mission of The Republic
    of Botswana to the UN
866 United Nations Plaza
New York, N.Y.

Brazil
Brazilian Government Trade
    Bureau
551 Fifth Avenue
New York, N.Y.

Bulgaria
Embassy of the People's
    Republic of Bulgaria
2100 Sixteenth Street, NW
Washington, D.C.

Burma
Consulate General of Burma
10 East Seventy-seventh Street
New York, N.Y.

Burundi
Permanent Mission of the Kingdom
    of Burundi to the UN
485 Fifth Avenue
New York, N.Y.

*Byelorussian Soviet Socialist
    Republic*
See Union of Soviet Socialist
    Republics

Cambodia
Permanent Mission of Cambodia
    to the UN
845 Third Avenue
New York, N.Y.

Cameroon
Permanent Mission of the Federal
    Republic of Cameroon to the UN
866 United Nations Plaza
New York, N.Y.

Canada
Consulate General of Canada
Press and Information Service
680 Fifth Avenue
New York, N.Y.

Central African Republic
Permanent Mission of the Central
    African Republic to the UN
386 Park Avenue South
New York, N.Y.

Ceylon
Embassy of Ceylon
2148 Wyoming Avenue, NW
Washington, D.C.

Chad
Permanent Mission of the Republic
    of Chad to the UN
150 East Fifty-second Street
New York, N.Y.

Chile
Consulate General of Chile
809 United Nations Plaza
New York, N.Y.

China
Chinese Information Service
100 West Thirty-second Street
New York, N.Y.

Colombia
Consulate General of Colombia
10 East Forty-sixth Street
New York, N.Y.

Congo (Brazzaville)
Permanent Mission of the
    Republic of the Congo
    (Brazzaville) to the UN
444 Madison Avenue
New York, N.Y.

Congo Democratic Republic
Permanent Mission of the
    Democratic Republic of the
    Congo to the UN
402 East Fifty-first Street
New York, N.Y.

Costa Rica
Permanent Mission of Costa Rica
    to the UN
211 East Forty-third Street
New York, N.Y.

Cuba
Permanent Mission of Cuba
    to the UN
6 East Sixty-seventh Street
New York, N.Y.

Cyprus
Permanent Mission of Cyprus
    to the UN
165 East Seventy-second Street
New York, N.Y.

Czechoslovakia
Embassy of the Czechoslovak
    Republic
3900 Linnean Avenue, NW
Washington, D.C.

Dahomey
Permanent Mission of the Republic
    of Dahomey to the UN
4 East Seventy-third Street
New York, N.Y.

Denmark
Danish Consulate General
280 Park Avenue
New York, N.Y.

Dominican Republic
Permanent Mission of the
    Dominican Republic to the UN
144 East Forty-fourth Street
New York, N.Y.

Ecuador
Consulate General of Ecuador
1270 Avenue of the Americas
New York, N.Y.

El Salvador
Consulate General of El Salvador
211 East Forty-third Street
New York, N.Y.

Ethiopia
Embassy of Ethiopia
2134 Kalorama Road, NW
Washington, D.C.

Finland
Finnish Consulate General
200 East Forty-second Street
New York, N.Y.

France
Embassy of France, Press and
    Information Division
972 Fifth Avenue
New York, N.Y.

Gabon
Permanent Mission of the
    Republic of Gabon to the UN
866 United Nations Plaza
New York, N.Y.

Gambia
Permanent Mission of Gambia
    to the UN
c/o Mission of Senegal
51 East Forty-second Street
New York, N.Y.

Ghana
Ghana Information and Trade
    Center
150 East Fifty-eighth Street
New York, N.Y.

Greece
Greek Consulate General
69 East Seventy-ninth Street
New York, N.Y.

Guatemala
Consulate General of Guatemala
1270 Avenue of the Americas
New York, N.Y.

Guinea
Embassy of Guinea
2112 Leroy Place, NW
Washington 8, D.C.

Guyana
Permanent Mission of Guyana
    to the UN
355 Lexington Avenue
New York, N.Y.

Haiti
Consulate General of Haiti
60 East Forty-second Street
New York, N.Y.

Honduras
Permanent Mission of Honduras
    to the UN
290 Madison Avenue
New York, N.Y.

Hungary
Permanent Mission of the
    Hungarian People's Republic
    to the UN
10 East Seventy-fifth Street
New York, N.Y.

Iceland
Consulate General of Iceland
420 Lexington Avenue
New York, N.Y.

India
Consulate General of India
3 East Sixty-fourth Street
New York, N.Y.

Indonesia
Consulate General of Indonesia
5 East Sixty-eighth Street
New York, N.Y.

Iran
Consulate General of Iran
630 Fifth Avenue
New York, N.Y.

Iraq
Permanent Mission of Iraq
    to the UN
c/o Press Officer
14 East Seventy-ninth Street
New York, N.Y.

Ireland
Consulate General of Ireland
580 Fifth Avenue
New York, N.Y.

Israel
The Israel Office of Information
11 East Seventieth Street
New York, N.Y.

Italy
Italian Cultural Institute
686 Park Avenue
New York, N.Y.

Ivory Coast
Permanent Mission of Ivory Coast
    to the UN
46 East Seventy-fourth Street
New York, N.Y.

Jamaica
Consulate General of Jamaica
Information Service
200 Park Avenue
New York, N.Y.

Japan
Japan Information Service
Consulate General of Japan
235 East Forty-second Street
New York, N.Y.

Jordan
Embassy of Jordan
2319 Wyoming Avenue, NW
Washington, D.C.

Kenya
Permanent Mission of the
    Republic of Kenya to the UN
866 United Nations Plaza
New York, N.Y.

Kuwait
Permanent Mission of Kuwait
    to the UN
235 East Forty-second Street
New York, N.Y.

Laos
Embassy of Laos
2222 S Street, NW
Washington, D.C.

Lebanon
Consulate General of Lebanon
9 East Seventy-sixth Street
New York, N.Y.

Liberia
Consulate General of Liberia
1120 Avenue of the Americas
New York, N.Y.

Libya
Embassy of Libya
2344 Massachusetts Avenue, NW
Washington, D.C.

Luxembourg
Consulate General of Luxembourg
200 East Forty-second Street
New York, N.Y.

Madagascar
Permanent Mission of the Malagasy
    Republic to the UN
301 East Forty-seventh Street
New York, N.Y.

Malawi
Permanent Mission of the Republic
    of Malawi to the UN
777 Third Avenue
New York, N.Y.

Malaysia
Permanent Mission of Malaysia
    to the UN
845 Third Avenue
New York, N.Y.

Mali
Permanent Mission of the Republic
    of Mali to the UN
111 East Sixty-ninth Street
New York, N.Y.

Malta
Permanent Mission of Malta
    to the UN
249 East Thirty-fifth Street
New York, N.Y.

Mauritania
Permanent Mission of the Islamic
  Republic of Mauritania to
  to the UN
8 West Fortieth Street
New York, N.Y.

Mauritius
Permanent Mission of Mauritius
  to the UN
301 East Forty-seventh Street
New York, N.Y.

Mexico
Mexican Consulate General
8 East Forty-first Street
New York, N.Y.

Mongolia
Permanent Mission of the
  Mongolian People's Republic
  to the UN
6 East Seventy-seventh Street
New York, N.Y.

Morocco
Embassy of Morocco
1601 Twenty-first Street, NW
Washington, D.C.

Nepal
Royal Nepalese Consulate General
300 East Forty-sixth Street
New York, N.Y.

Netherlands
Netherlands Information Service
711 Third Avenue
New York, N.Y.

New Zealand
Consulate General of New Zealand
630 Fifth Avenue
New York, N.Y.

Nicaragua
Consulate General of Nicaragua
Room 1813
1270 Avenue of the Americas
New York, N.Y.

Niger
Permanent Mission of Niger
  to the UN
Suite 570
866 United Nations Plaza
New York, N.Y.

Nigeria
Permanent Mission of Nigeria
  to the UN
757 Third Avenue
New York, N.Y.

Norway
Norwegian Information Service
825 Third Avenue
New York, N.Y.

Pakistan
Permanent Mission of Pakistan
  to the UN
8 East Sixty-fifth STreet
New York, N.Y.

Panama
Consulate General of Panama
12 East Sixty-fifth Street
New York, N.Y.

Paraguay
Permanent Mission of Paraguay
  to the UN
211 East Forty-third Street
New York, N.Y.

Peru
Consulate General of Peru
10 Rockefeller Plaza
New York, N.Y.

Philippines
Consulate General of the
  Philippines
15 East Sixty-sixth Street
New York, N.Y.

Poland
Embassy of the Polish People's
  Republic
2640 Sixteenth Street, NW
Washington, D.C.

Portugal
Casa de Portugal
570 Fifth Avenue
New York, N.Y.

Rumania
Embassy of the Socialist Republic
   of Rumania
1607 Twenty-third Street, NE
Washington, D.C.

Rwanda
Permanent Mission of the
   Rwandese Republic to the UN
Room 630
120 East Fifty-sixth Street
New York, N.Y.

Saudi Arabia
Saudi Arabian Consulate General
Room 527
866 United Nations Plaza
New York, N.Y.

Senegal
Permanent Mission of the Republic
   of Senegal to the UN
51 East Forty-second Street
New York, N.Y.

Sierra Leone
Consulate General of Sierra Leone
Room 609
30 East Forty-second Street
New York, N.Y.

Singapore
Permanent Mission of Singapore
   to the UN
711 Third Avenue
New York, N.Y.

Somalia
Permanent Mission of Somalia
   to the UN
236 East Forty-sixth Street
New York, N.Y.

South Africa
South African Information Service
655 Madison Avenue
New York, N.Y.

Southern Yemen
Permanent Mission of the People's
   Republic of Southern Yemen
   to the UN
Room 427
866 United Nations Plaza
New York, N.Y.

Spain
Embassy of Spain
Office of the Cultural Counselor
2700 Fifteenth Street, NW
Washington, D.C.

Sudan
Permanent Mission of the Republic
   of Sudan to the UN
757 Third Avenue
New York, N.Y.

Swaziland
Permanent Mission of the Kingdom
   of Swaziland to the UN
141 East Forty-fourth Street
New York, N.Y.

Sweden
Swedish Information Service
825 Third Avenue
New York, N.Y.

Syria
Permanent Mission of the Syrian
   Arab Republic to the UN
Room 2505
150 East Fifty-eighth Street
New York, N.Y.

Thailand
Embassy of Thailand
2300 Kalorama Road
Washington, D.C.

Togo
Permanent Mission of Togo
   to the UN
Room 400
800 Second Avenue
New York, N.Y.

Trinidad and Tobago
Embassy of Trinidad and Tobago
2209 Massachusetts Avenue
Washington, D.C.

Tunisia
Trade and Tourist Office
Room 2918
Pan Am Building
200 Park Avenue
New York, N.Y.

Turkey
Turkish Government Tourism and
    Information Office
500 Fifth Avenue
New York, N.Y.

Uganda
Permanent Mission of Uganda
    to the UN
801 Second Avenue
New York, N.Y.

Ukrainian Soviet Socialist Republic
See Union of Soviet Socialist
    Republics

Union of Soviet Socialist Republics
Permanent Mission of Union of
    Soviet Socialist Republics
    to the UN
136 East Sixty-seventh Street
New York, N.Y.

United Arab Republic
Permanent Mission of United Arab
    Republic to the UN
36 East Sixty-seventh Street
New York, N.Y.

United Kingdom
British Information Services
845 Third Avenue
New York, N.Y.

United Republic of Tanzania
Permanent Mission of the United
    Republic of Tanzania to the UN
800 Second Avenue
New York, N.Y.

United States
Department of State
Public Services Division
Washington, D.C.

Upper Volta
Permanent Mission of the Republic
    of Upper Volta to the UN
866 Second Avenue, East
New York, N.Y.

Uruguay
Consulate General of Uruguay
17 Battery Place
New York, N.Y.

Venezuela
Consulate General of Venezuela
600 Fifth Avenue
New York, N.Y.

Yemen
Permanent Mission of the Arab
    Republic of Yemen to the UN
211 East Forty-third Street
New York, N.Y.

Yugoslavia
Yugoslavia Information Center
488 Madison Avenue
New York, N.Y.

Zambia
Permanent Mission of the Republic
    of Zambia
150 East Fifty-eighth Street
New York, N.Y.

INFORMATION SERVICES OF ACCREDITED OBSERVERS AND NONMEMBER STATES IN THE UNITED NATIONS

Germany (Federal Republic)
German Consulate General
460 Park Avenue
New York, N.Y.

Holy See
Office of the Permanent Observer
of the Holy See to the UN
c/o Holy Family Church
315 East Forty-seventh Street
New York, N.Y.

Korea
Consulate General of Korea
9 East Eightieth Street
New York, N.Y.

Monaco
Monaco Information Center
610 Fifth Avenue
New York, N.Y.

Switzerland
Consulate General of
Switzerland
444 Madison Avenue
New York, N.Y.

Vietnam
Office of the Permanent Observer
of Vietnam to the UN
866 United Nations Plaza
New York, N.Y.

Discussion and Debate

Discussion is an area of speech that is receiving an increased amount of attention, undoubtedly because it is the most natural form of communication. Acquaintances get together for lunch or parties, committees are formed every day, and family members talk to each other. For the purposes of speech students, however, a discussion occurs when two or more persons purposely set out to solve a problem or to clarify ideas. Theoretically, a group will produce more ideas and solutions so that the end result will be better thought out than if only an individual had arrived at it.

THE MEETING

Group Meeting

Organized informal discussions are composed of not more than twenty members, usually guided by a leader, speaking on subjects of mutual interest. For some groups, cooperative investigations are more formal and have a more definite purpose. Group members research subtopics, present the information, and then attempt to arrive at a solution, which may take more than one meeting. Boards of education, city councils, and church boards are examples of groups that tend to use this method. Committees and conferences facilitate decision-making by having an odd number of people in the group. Business meetings are ideally composed of all the members of the organization. They follow the rules of parliamentary procedure and most of the speaking consists of statements for or against a certain motion. The leader, who functions more formally than do the leaders in other group discussions, enforces the parliamentary rules and follows a strict agenda.

Public Meetings

Public discussion meetings are more formal than group meetings and have large audiences with only a few people speaking. The leader, instead of participating in the discussion, functions as a moderator, introducing the speakers and calling for audience questions. The major types of public discussions are the panel-forum, symposium-forum, lecture-forum and debate-forum.

The *panel-forum* is designed to inform the audience so that it can take action on a problem. Panels usually consist of a chairman and from three to six experts with diverse views who interact with each other. The *symposium-forum* differs from the panel in that it is more presentational than conversational. It is composed of a moderator and three or four others who are well informed and present divergent views directly to the audience. The *lecture-forum* consists of one expert speaking on a subject for a given amount of time. The *debate-forum,* unlike the panel, symposium or lecture, moves from providing information to the advocacy of a solution to a problem. It provides an intensive examination of the pros and cons of one specific proposal or solution to a problem.

Traditional school debates have two people on each side, while public debates usually have one person representing each point of view. The affirmative speaker proposes and supports the solution to the problem and the negative speaker opposes the solution. There is a strict time limit set for each presentation. For instance, the chairman may make a three-minute introduction, the affirmative speaker presents his case for twenty minutes, the negative speaker gives his arguments for twenty-five minutes, and the affirmative is allowed a five-minute rebuttal.

Educational debate procedures vary somewhat. One of the

most widely used patterns for speaking order and time limits consists of the following: Of the constructive speeches, the first and second affirmative and the first and second negative speakers, who speak alternately, all get ten minutes; rebuttal speeches are all five minutes long, the order consisting of first negative, first affirmative, second negative, and second affirmative speakers.

Cross-examination debating has a different schedule and, in order to learn about it and about how to prepare the affirmative and negative cases, a speaker should refer to books specializing in debate found on pages 139-140. The *forum* sections of all these discussions consist of the question-answer session with the audience, which normally appears at the end of the discussions.

PROBLEMS AND ROLES

Discussion Problems

Problems for group discussions must not be so simple that the solution may be arrived at with little or no exchange of ideas and opinions. They must be within the intellectual scope of the group members and narrow enough in scope so that a solution may be arrived at in the time allotted. Wording should be concrete and it should be phrased preferably in the form of a question.

Role of the Leader

The leader has a significant role in most of these discussion forms. He sets the tone, introduces the subject matter and the speakers, and gives the agenda and procedure. In more informal discussions where there is interaction between people, he must be able to handle the various types of people—i.e. encourage silent ones to talk, discourage one member from taking over the discussion, smooth over any hostilities, etc. He must keep the goal in mind and not allow any digressions. At the end of the discussion, it is his duty to handle audience questions and direct them to the appropriate expert, to objectively sum up what has been said, state any solutions or recommendations in a clear-cut style, and make any necessary concluding remarks.

Speaking on Radio and Television

During the last few decades, a revolution has occurred in the field of communication. No longer must speakers meet their audiences face to face. In this age of mass media, speakers reach larger audiences faster than ever before, but may never experience any immediate feedback. Microphones of radio and television send out the verbal message, and television cameras transmit the speaker's image without allowing the speaker to see his audience. This results in special problems for the speaker. He cannot know what type of audience he is speaking to or if he is losing them. Therefore, even more time must be spent in preparation, because the speech must be more attention-getting and clear-cut than it would normally be. Because people tune in at different times, the topic and major ideas of a speech or discussion must also be restated more frequently.

Radio speakers are especially limited in that the whole burden of presentation is relegated to the voice; therefore, it must be especially versatile and pleasing. Both radio and television speakers must remember the audience's setting and gauge their voices accordingly. The audience members are in their own homes, not in large lecture halls, so the tone should be natural and conversational. Extraneous noises are more distracting on radio and television because the microphones pick up every sound. The speaker should not rustle the pages of his speech, breathe heavily, or clear his throat into the microphone. Microphones should be kept at the same distance from the speaker throughout the speech or else the voice volume may change too dramatically without motivation from the speech context. Most radio and television speakers must also allow for commercial breaks and time their speeches more strictly than would a regular speaker. Otherwise, the general rules as discussed in this research guide apply to radio and television speakers and broadcasters, as well as to any speaker meeting his audience face to face.

Oral Interpretation of Literature, Group Reading, and Readers' Theater

ORAL INTERPRETATION OF LITERATURE

It differs from oratory, debate, or discussion in that none of the material is composed by the speaker, except perhaps for a short, explanatory introduction. Thus, the only alterations made will be ones that eliminate cumbersome sentence construction—particularly in quotations. For example: "The question is," said Humpty Dumpty, "which is to be master—that's all"—in which the clause "said Humpty Dumpty" may be cut out, leaving the sense to be implied by the speaker's voice. His major role is to communicate to the best of his ability another author's ideas and feelings. This involves a capability to analyze a literary work and determine its underlying action, theme, climaxes, and symbols. All of the words and images must be thoroughly understood. Imagination is necessary to visualize the scene or setting and to personify any characters without resorting to pantomime or overacting. Movement and voice must function together clearly to convey the symbolic meaning and mood, to enhance comprehension, and to stimulate the audience's imaginations so that they will be able to empathize with and visualize the characters, setting, and theme.

GROUP READING AND READERS' THEATER

Many voices may obtain a greater variety of effects than solo oral interpretation of literature because there can be more use of symbolic movement and vocal variations to communicate the underlying conflict, action, and meaning. Normally speaking, in these areas one leader analyzes the literature and directs the movement and voices of the group. A knowledge of the theater might be particularly valuable to students interested in this area of speech.

Part IV

THE HISTORY OF ORATORY: A REVIEW

The History of Oratory

INTRODUCTION

It is impossible to review the history of public speaking without getting one's definitions in good working order first. If you are hunting for a good summary of the art of public speaking in an encyclopaedia, you will probably not find it under "p" for public but under "o" for oratory. No sooner have you made this discovery than you will be informed by the writer of the article that in Greece and Rome oratory was considered a part of rhetoric—that is the art of composing as well as delivering a speech. In the Middle Ages rhetoric was one of the trivium (with logic and grammar) that made up the study of the liberal arts. It was not until early modern times that oratory was used to mean public speaking and rhetoric reserved to describe the art of composition only. And then, to totally confuse matters, the word oratory gave way to the more descriptive phrase, "public speaking." Some authorities also like to point out that public speaking describes a less formal delivery than the carefully ordered, stately rhythms encouraged by the ancient teachers of rhetoric . . . and oratory.

Be that as it may, the history of oratory is, in essence, the history of mankind's most fundamental form of communication. Tracing the history of oratory-public speaking is a short course in the ceaseless effort of men to persuade their fellow men—often with dramatic and important consequences for the generations that followed.

The table (table 7) that follows is a broad outline of the

major speakers, their speeches, and reasons for speaking from the first Greek rhetoricians to our own 'public speakers.' Limitations of space made it impossible to mention every speaker of note, or to list all the representative speeches. The chart is, instead, a starting point for students interested in the evolution of persuasive public speech. Students interested in improving their own mastery of public speaking may wish to obtain copies of the speeches cited in the chart and practice saying them. There are many precedents for this activity: such early American leaders as Adams and Jefferson regularly rehearsed Cicero's speeches in the privacy of their homes so that they would be more effective in public. In sum, a review of the history of oratory is valuable both for the historian of ideas and the future maker of ideas.

TABLE 7 Great Speakers and Their Speeches

Period	Speaker	Major Speeches or Works	Characteristics and Significance
THE CLASSICAL RHETORI-CIANS c. 500 B.C. to c. 500 A.D. The Greeks	Pericles c. 500-429 B.C.	"Funeral Oration for the Athenians" 430 B.C.	Athenian statesman whose aim was to make Athens a perfect democracy and the leading Greek city-state. Attempts to unite Greece failed, the Peloponnesian War followed, and Pericles' most famous speech is a eulogy of the Athenians who fell in first year of war.
	Gorgias c. 485-375 B.C.	"For the Union of Greek States against Persia"* Eulogy of Helen*	A Sicilian-born rhetorician and sophist (wise man and teacher) for whom one of Plato's dialogues is named. Emphasized beautiful expression in speech, broke up sentences into short, balanced clauses. Had students memorize great speeches and parts of great literary works for practice.
	Antiphon c. 480-411 B.C.	"On the Murder of Herodes"* and about 14 other works	Athenian orator, author of speeches for others to deliver, and teacher of rhetoric; work characterized by simple, direct legal style. Executed for his part in conspiracy to establish less democratic government in Athens.
	Protagoras c. 480-c. 410 B.C.	Four fragments survive. Best known for statement, "Man is the measure of all things."*	Sophist immortalized in Plato's dialogue of the same name. Philosophy based on agnosticism; stated that since each man is the evaluator of truth, truth can only by judged in terms of the man.
	Corax 5th Century B.C. (exact dates unknown)	No works have survived. _____ *Exact date unknown	A Sicilian teacher of rhetoric said to have made rules for oratory that divided speech into five parts: 1) Proem or prologue, 2) Narrative arguments, 3) Subsidiary remarks, 4) Peroration, or summing up, and, 5) Conclusion, indicating probable results of argument set forth in speech.

TABLE 7 / Great Speakers and Their Speeches *continued*

Period	Speaker	Major Speeches or Works	Characteristics and Significance
	Isocrates 436-338 B.C.	"Busiris" and "Encomiam on Helen," rhetorical critiques.* "Evagoras," an encomiam on a king.* "Panathenaicus" a written review in praise of Athens' history.* "Panegyricus" (festival oration) urging union of Athens and Sparta against Persia.*	Shyness and weak voice kept Isocrates out of public life but he was known as supporter of democracy and founder of a famous school in Athens, mentioned in Plato's *Phaedrus,* Isocrates was influenced by Gorgias (see above) and was with him one of the first to make an art of rhetoric. His speeches are elegant and highly stylized, as he used such devices as antithesis (contrast) and long, swelling phrases.
	Plato c. 427-348 B.C.	*Gorgias** *Phaedrus** *Protagoras** *The Republic**	Student of Socrates, considered by many the greatest Greek philosopher. Plato thought the spoken word superior to the written, but none of his speeches have survived. His views can be gathered from his books and references in Aristotle's writing. Considered rhetoric a means of communicating reality through dialectical exposition.
	Aristotle 384-322 B.C.	*Organon** *De Anima** *Nichomachean Ethics** *Rhetoric**	Student of Plato, later teacher of Alexander the Great, and then directed Lyceum, a school in Athens. One of the giants of philosophy, Aristotle devised the syllogism and made a science out of the process of reasoning (see the *Organon*); explored psychology (*De Anima*); taught that ethics was a part of politics (*Nicomachean Ethics*), and organized the principles of persuasion through the spoken and written word (*Rhetoric*). Rhetorical principles analyzed by Aristotle examined how speaker could convince audience of his own worth, how to arouse the listeners, and the various methods of arguing a point. All his works influenced development of western thought.
		*Exact date unknown	

TABLE 7 / Great Speakers and Their Speeches *continued*

Period	Speaker	Major Speeches or Works	Characteristics and Significance
	Demosthenes 383-322 B.C.	"First Philippic" 351 B.C. "On the Peace" 346 B.C. "Second Philippic" 344 B.C. "On the Embassy" 343 B.C. "On the Chersonese" 341 B.C. "Third Philippic" 341 B.C. "On the Crown" 330 B.C.	Called the greatest Greek orator, he combined exalted ideas with simple, direct speech. Could evoke all the emotions in a single speech, but his aim was always persuasion, never artistic speech for its own sake. Advocated strong resistance on part of Athenians against Philip of Macedon. Some of these speeches are known as philippics, a word still used to describe an invective speech. "On the Crown" considered his masterpiece, was essentially defense of his own political acts.
The Romans	Marcus Porcius Cato 234-149 B.C.	Only fragments survive, *De Agri Culture*—oldest surviving Latin prose work.*	Roman statesman, attacked luxury and laxness of wealthy Romans and hoped for a return to a simpler agricultural way of life. Particularly known for his concern over danger to Rome from Carthage in North Africa and warned that *"Cartago delenda est"*—"Carthage must be destroyed." Speeches were marked by honesty, simplicity, wit, and directness.
	The Gracchi: Tiberius Sempronius Gracchus (d. 133 B.C.) Gaius Sempronius Gracchus (d. 121 B.C.)	"The People's Rights Above Privilege" c. 121 B.C. (Gaius)	Brothers best known for efforts to solve economic problems arising from unfair distribution of farm land. Both known to have been influenced in speaking style by Greeks. Latin rhetorical art sometimes said to have begun with Gracchi.
	Marcus Tullius Cicero 106-43 B.C.	"Against Verres" 70 B.C. "Orations Against Catiline" 63 B.C. _____ *Exact date unknown	Roman statesman and greatest orator of his age, even his enemy Antony (against whom Philippics were directed) called him eloquent. Earliest important speech directed against evil governor of Sicily.

TABLE 7 / Great Speakers and Their Speeches *continued*

Period	*Speaker*	*Major Speeches or Works*	*Characteristics and Significance*
		14 "Philippics" 44-43 B.C. *De Oratore* (Of Oratory) *Brutus* c. 45 B.C. *Orator* c. 45 B.C.	Catiline led a conspiracy against government that Cicero attacked. The three books listed are handbooks and a history of rhetoric. His love of liberty and his mastery of the complete range of emotions in oratory gained him lasting fame.
	Quintilian (Marcus Fabius Quintilianus) c. A.D. 35-c. 95	*Institutes of Oratory**	Quintilian, who was born in Spain, became the first teacher of rhetoric in Rome to receive an official salary. His fame and wealth as a teacher and as an advocate in courts made an early retirement possible. Spent last years writing *Institutes*, which were influential in his own day and as late as the Renaissance, when his belief that education should build a man of character and broad culture was highly acclaimed and emulated.
THE EARLY CHURCH — A.D. 600	Jesus of Nazareth	"Sermon on the Mount" The Parables	Both in his long sermons and the briefer illustrative stories called parables, Jesus spoke simply and directly so that even the least among his listeners could understand the message of God's love.
	Saint Paul d. A.D. 67 ?	*First and 2nd Thessalonians* A.D. 62	The greatest missionary Apostle of the early Church, decisive in the formation of Christian faith. All works marked by fervent spirit of the Apostle.
	Saint Gregory Thaumaturgus (Wonder-worker) c. 213-c. 268	"Panegyric on Origen"* _____ *Exact date unknown	Greek bishop of Neocaesarea, said to have converted his whole diocese to the faith. Known for his devotion to his friend and teacher, Origen, the Christian philosopher who died as a result of persecution, and whom Gregory eulogized.

TABLE 7 / Great Speakers and Their Speeches *continued*

Period	Speaker	Major Speeches or Works	Characteristics and Significance
	Saint Basil the Great c. 330-379	*Longer* and *Shorter Rule for Basilian Monks** *Homilies** *Against Eunomius** *On The Holy Ghost**	Father of the Greek Church. Reported to have delivered forceful, clear, logical, and eloquent sermons. Monastic rules influenced St. Benedict. Written works noted for clarity and eloquence in their defense of faith.
	Saint Ambrose 340?-397	"On the Role of The Emperor"* *On the Duties of the Clergy** *On the Christian Faith**	Bishop of Milan, Doctor of the Church, chief opponent of Arian heresy in the West. Defined role of emperor as "in the Church, not above it." Works reveal deep study of Roman classics (notably Cicero) and of Christian documents. Used allegory to instruct.
	Saint John Chrysostom (Golden-Mouth) c. 347-407	"In Defense of Eutropius" c. 402 Homilies	Doctor of the Church, considered greatest of the Greek fathers. As patriarch of Constantinople, acted to reform clergy. Exiled for defense of Eutropius, whom he said was accused falsely. In that speech and brilliant homilies, won acclaim for his eloquence.
	Saint Augustine 354-430	*Confessions* c. 400 *City of God* c. 412 *On the Trinity**	Doctor of the Church, one of the four Latin fathers, Bishop of Hippo (North Africa). Before his conversion, had been a student and teacher of rhetoric. Considered a master of style and one of the great philosophers of all time.
	Saint Gregory the Great c. 540-604	*Morals on the Book of Job** *Dialogues** *Pastoral Care** Homilies on the Gospel ———— *Exact date unknown	Pope (590-604) and Doctor of the Church, led Catholics in time of upheaval and warfare. Strengthened temporal, as well as spiritual, side of the Church. Spoke and wrote with great clarity, made use of allegories to convey his ideas.

TABLE 7 / Great Speakers and Their Speeches continued

Period	Speaker	Major Speeches or Works	Characteristics and Significance
THE MIDDLE AGES c. 600-1300	Bede, St. Bede, or the Venerable Bede 673-735.	"Sermon on all Saints" 710? *History of the Abbots* * *Ecclesiastical History of the English Nation* *	An English monk of the Benedictine order. Works, notably *Ecclesiastical History*, invaluable source for information on his epoch. Writings marked by clarity; use of homilies and allegories in sermons.
	Saint Bernard of Clairvaux 1090?-1153	"Sermons on the Canticles" collected in *St. Bernard On the Song of Songs* * *On the Steps of Humility and Pride* c. 1125 *On the Love of God* c. 1127	French churchman, Doctor of the Church, mystic who was renowned for his miraculous cures, wisdom, and eloquence. Life devoted to betterment of Church, Cistercian order of monks, and good of mankind. Called "The Melli022fluous Doctor" because of his strong oratorical style, rich in allusions to Bible, but direct and personal in delivery.
	Peter Abelard 1079-1142	*Sic et non* (Yes and no) *	French teacher and philosopher who adopted Aristotelian logic to demonstrate truths of faith, which led to a conflict with St. Bernard of Clairvaux, whose mysticism denied necessity for such logical proofs. Abelard's brilliance as a lecturer attracted many students and he is sometimes called founder of University of Paris.
	Saint Thomas Aquinas 1225-1274	*Commentary in the Sentences* 1254-56 *Summa Theologica* 1267-73	Called the "Angelic Doctor," this Italian-born philosopher is one of the principal Roman Catholic saints and the greatest scholastic philosopher. Slow movements coupled with a brilliant, sharp mind made him an outstanding lecturer (see the *Commentary*—a collection of lectures). The *Summa* is a summary of his philosophical and theological views.
		*Exact date unknown	

TABLE 7 / Great Speakers and Their Speeches *continued*

Period	Speaker	Major Speeches or Works	Characteristics and Significance
THE REFORMA-TION 1300-1600	John Wyclif c. 1328-1384 (England)	"Sermon on Prayer" and many other works available in collected editions.	One of the earliest religious leaders to protest against abuses of Church, called "Morning Star of the Reformation." Associated with Wyclif Bible, first English translation of Latin Vulgate. Taught through sermons delivered in the vernacular. Centered sermons on a theme and was logical, practical, and popular.
	John Huss 1369-1415 (Bohemia, now Czechoslovakia)	*De ecclesia* (of the Church)* *Letters**	Priest, rector of Charles University in Prague, follower of Wyclif, and one of the great early reformers. Known for his use of Czech in place of Latin in sermons and hymns, condemnation of idea of infallibility of immoral popes, and efforts to restore Church to early ideas of poverty and brotherhood. Declared a heretic and burned at the stake.
	Girolamo Savonarola 1452-1498 (Italy)	*On the Degeneration of the Church**	A Dominican monk of extraordinary eloquence, he bitterly attacked corruption of Church and savagely denounced vanity of the people of Florence. Burned at the stake.
	Desiderius Erasmus 1466?-1536 (The Netherlands)	*Proverbs* 1500 *Manual of the Christian Knight* 1503 *The Praise of Folly* 1509 *The Education of a Christian Prince* 1515 *Colloquies* 1516	A priest and a great classical scholar, he denounced the abuses of the Church, but deplored the excesses of the religious war of his time. In his writing, one can see the sharply critical and satirical phrases that made him one of the leaders of his age.
	Martin Luther 1483-1546 (Germany)	Lectures on Paul 1513 Disputation with Johann Eck 1519 _____ *Exact date unknown	Leader of the Reformation in Germany. An ordained priest, he protested sale of indulgences and eventually broke with Church of Rome. Urged German control

TABLE 7 / Great Speakers and Their Speeches *continued*

Period	Speaker	Major Speeches or Works	Characteristics and Significance
		Address to the Nobility of The German Nation 1520 Defense Before the Diet of Worms 1521	of Church in Germany and asked for help of nation's princes. Attacked papal supremacy, corruption in Church, usury. Believe in justification by faith alone. Excommunicated in 1521 and presented views to Diet of Worms. Later translated Bible into German. Forceful sermons and writing helped him establish church named for him.
	John Knox 1505?-1572 (Scotland)	"Admonition" 1554 *First Blast of the Trumpet Against the Monstrous Regiment of Women* 1588 *"Against Tyrants"* 1565	Priest of Roman Catholic Church who later became founder of Scottish Presbyterianism. Known for hostility to Queen Mary of England and other "tyrants," he lived many years in Geneva, influenced Calvin, and through his zeal and fiery sermons, converted many to new mode of worship.
	Huldreich Zwingli 1484-1531 (Switzerland)	Lectures on the New Testament 1519 *Architeles* 1522 67 Theses 1523	Influence of Erasmus and democratic life of Swiss cantons led him to renounce Church. Lectures on New Testament considered beginning of Reformation in Switzerland. In *Architeles*, announced his belief in freedom of local churches from Rome. Argued his belief with papal representative in clear, forceful theses at Zurich Council and was upheld by council. His church established in that city.
	John Calvin 1509-1564 (France)	*Institutes of the Christian Religion* 1536 Sermon "On Enduring Persecution" 1552	One of the major figures in the Protestant Reformation, Calvin experienced a "sudden conversion" and systematized ideas in the *Institutes*. Preached austerity and reform from his pulpit in Geneva, where he briefly established a theocratic government. Emphasis on thrift, industry, responsibility, regarded as preparing his followers for participating in Industrial Revolution.

TABLE 7 / Great Speakers and Their Speeches *continued*

Period	Speaker	Major Speeches or Works	Characteristics and Significance
THE COUNTER-REFORMA-TION 1450-1750	Saint Ignatius of Loyola, 1491-1556 (Spain)	*Formula* (for Society) 1539 *Spiritual Exercises*	Founder of the Society of Jesus (Jesuits), Saint Ignatius emphasized spirituality, the education of young people, and the establishment of foreign missions to convert pagans to the faith. *Spiritual Exercises* reflect his mysticism and express ways of reaching God.
	Saint Charles Borromeo 1538-1584 (Italy)	Sermons**	A Church leader who personally exem-plified spirit of ascetism that he hoped would restrengthen Church. In strong sermons urged his ways on priests, some of whom felt he was too strict.
	Saint Theresa of Avila 1515-1582 (Spain)	*Life* 1562-65 *Ways of Perfection* c. 1565 *Interior Castle* *Foundations* 1573-82 *Exclamations of the Soul to God* 1569	A leading Roman Catholic saint, Theresa of Avila worked, traveled, preached, persuaded, and wrote tire-lessly. Used a simple, spiritual, but blunt style, rich in metaphors. St. Theresa was one of the leaders of the Counter-Reformation and one of the great mystics of all time.
	Saint John of the Cross 1542-1591 (Spain)	*Spiritual Canticle* c. 1577 *The Dark Night of the Soul.**	A follower of St. Theresa, this mystic founded the order of Discalced Carmel-ites and is considered one of the greatest Spanish lyric poets.
	Jacques Bénigne Bossuet 1627-1704 (France)	"Funeral Oration on the Prince de Conde" and other *Funeral Orations* 1689, *Exposition of Catholic Doctrine* 1671	Roman Catholic priest, considered one of the leading orators of the age and particularly renowned for his funeral orations, in which he combined grace, self-control, eloquence, and restrained power. Moral, stylistically graceful, and a brilliant debator.
		**various dates *exact dates unknown.	

TABLE 7 / Great Speakers and Their Speeches *continued*

Period	Speaker	Major Speeches or Works	Characteristics and Significance
FRANCE—THROUGH AGE OF NAPOLEON 1749-1815	Honore Gabriel Riquetti, Comte de Mirabeau 1749-91	"And Yet You Deliber-ate" 1789 "Against the Nobility and Clergy of Province" 1789 "Reason Immutable and Sovereign" 1790 "Justifying Revolution" 1790 "In Defense of Himself" 1790	Revolutionist and statesman who aimed at establishing a constitutional monarchy. Although he did not write all speeches alone, they are notable for strength, subtlety, effective arrangement.
	Pierre Victurnien Vergniaud 1753-1793	"The State of the French Peasantry" 1789 "The Trial of the King" 1792 "The Call to Arms" 1792 "On the Situation in France" 1792	Revolutionist, leader of Girondists, re-nowned for oratory of great brilliance and power, laced with classical refer-ences. Guillotined by extremists.
	Maximilien François Marie Isidore de Robespierre 1758-1794	"Against Giving the King a Trial" 1792 "Last Speech" 1794	Revolutionist, leader of France (1793-94), led movement to have king killed and was responsible for Reign of Terror, which ended with his death. An eloquent, passionate, subtle speaker with a gift for extemporaneous address.
	George Jacques Danton 1759-1794	"To Dare, To Dare Again; Always to Dare" 1792 "Freedom of Worship" 1793	Leader of a revolutionary group called Cordeliers, he urged extreme action against foreign enemies in "To Dare." Later became leader of Jacobins who aimed for freedom and stable govern-ment. Executed by more radical wing in Reign of Terror. Speeches marked by violence and simplicity.

TABLE 7 / Great Speakers and Their Speeches *continued*

Period	Speaker	Major Speeches or Works	Characteristics and Significance
	Napoleon I (Bonaparte) 1769-1821	"To the Soldiers on Entering Milan" 1796 "Farewell to the Old Guard" 1814	General, political leader, later Emperor of France. One of the leading military orators of all time, he used short, energetic, powerful sentences to praise and urge his soldiers on.
ENGLAND 1525 to 1900	Thomas Wilson 1525?-1581	*Art of Rhetorique* 1553	Author of the first complete work on rhetoric in English, as well as the first English translations of Demosthenes (see above). Highly mannered style was extremely influential.
	Sir Edward Coke 1552-1634	"The Charges in Raleigh's Case" 1603 *Reports* 1600-15 *Institutes* 1628-44	Jurist, upholder of the common law, and opponent of royal rights and privilege. Speech and writings known for strength, courage, and tact.
	John Lyly 1554?-1606	*The Anatomy of Wit* 1578 *Euphues and His England* 1580	Playwright and prose writer, whose remarkable, elaborate style is best remembered as "euphuism," in which similes and illustrations, balanced phrases, alliteration, and antithesis were used. Euphuism now means a mannered style in which balanced phrases predominate.
	Oliver Cromwell 1599-1658	"At the Opening of Parliament under the Protectorate" 1654	Founder of the Protectorate, his energetic, vehement, militant speeches are notable for their sincerity and conviction.
	Sir Robert Walpole 1676-1745	*The Case of Mr. Walpole* (pamphlet) 1711 On the Peerage Bill 1718 Proposal on the South Sea Stock 1720 On Friendship with France 1727	Leading Whig statesman whose gifts as a leader, politician, and orator helped bring about decline of royal power and rise in influence of cabinet and parliament. Speeches simple, direct, satirical, colloquial, and often conversational. A master at debate.

TABLE 7 / Great Speakers and Their Speeches *continued*

Period	Speaker	Major Speeches or Works	Characteristics and Significance
	Philip Dormer Stanhope, Fourth Earl of Chester-field 1694-1773	"Against the Licensing Act" 1737 "Against the Gin Bill" 1743 *Letters to His Son* 1774	An opponent of Walpole whose speeches are noted for grace, wit, and sarcasm. Style can be best appreciated in his letters to his illegitimate son.
	John Wesley 1703-1791	"God's Love to Fallen Man"* "The Poverty of Reason"* *Journals* (1735-90)	Founder of Methodism, traveled widely in England and to Georgia, where he spread his belief that the grace of God could transform everyone's life who would accept it. Preached in open air because churches often closed to him. Spoke with great clarity, cogency, and personal conviction. Members of audience said they felt each word of Wesley's aimed at them personally.
	William Murray, First Earl of Mansfield 1705-1793	"On the Right to Tax America" 1766	Judge, parliamentarian, and organizer of modern foundations of commercial law. Spoke with logical, unemotional precision in an ethical and dignified way.
	William Pitt, First Earl of Chatham 1708-1778	"Retort to Walpole" 1741 "On the Right to Tax America" 1766 "On the War in America" 1777	Called "The Great Commoner," opposed Walpole. Favored conciliation of colonies, but not their independence. Ushered in new age of oratory through literary flavor of his forceful, witty, eloquent, formal speeches in Parliament.
	George Whitefield 1714-1770	"On the Method of Grace"* "The Kingdom of God"*	Associate of Wesley's in religious revival called "The Great Awakening." Sermons notable for simplicity, use of colloquial English, effective and dramatic blend of voice and action.
	Edmund Burke 1729-1797	"On American Taxation" 1774 ——————————— *Exact date unknown	Dublin-born writer and statesman who opposed king's actions toward American

TABLE 7 / Great Speakers and Their Speeches *continued*

Period	Speaker	Major Speeches or Works	Characteristics and Significance
		"On Conciliation of America" 1775 "Principles in Politics" 1780 "At the Trial of Warren Hastings" 1788 *Reflections on the Revolution in France* 1790	colonies, and Hasting's rule in India. Opposed French Revolution, however, and is considered spokesman of Conservatism. Often described as a great orator because of his ideas, but rapid pace of speech, brogue, and clumsy gestures made him difficult to listen to.
	Charles Fox 1749-1806	"On The British Defeat in America" 1780 "The Tyranny of the East India Company" 1783 "The Foreign Policy of Washington" 1794 "On the Refusal to Negotiate with France" 1800	An opponent of Pitt, he has been called the world's greatest debater because of his gift for extemporaneous speech. Favored liberal reform, conciliation of colonies, French Revolution, end of slave trade.
	William Pitt 1759-1806	"The War in America Denounced" 1781 "On an Attempt to Force his Resignation" 1784 Indicts the Slave Trade & Foresees a Liberated Africa 1792 "On the Refusal to Negotiate with France" 1800	Son of the First Earl of Chatham (see above), a statesman who was a liberal Tory up to the French Revolution. Threat from France caused him to suppress certain rights and also to misjudge French armed power. Brought about union of England and Ireland. Speeches during long parliamentary career noted for eloquence and effective use of attention-getting devices.
	John Thelwall 1764-1834	*Illustrations of English Rhythmus* * ——— *Exact date unknown	Foremost teacher of oratory and elocution of his time. Opening of school in 1801 caused a sensation. He studied and analyzed pupil's delivery, stressed voice production and control. Believed in rhythmic delivery.

TABLE 7 / Great Speakers and Their Speeches *continued*

Period	Speaker	Major Speeches or Works	Characteristics and Significance
	John Henry, Cardinal Newman 1801-1890	*Apologia pro Vita Sua* 1864 *Grammar of Assent* 1870	A convert to Catholicism and its leading spokesman in 19th-century England, Newman's sermons noted for their suavity, urbanity, and use of irony but best remembered for persuasiveness and understatement. Characteristics faithfully mirrored in his classic *Apology* and his logical exposition of faith, the *Grammar*.
	Benjamin Disraeli 1804-1881	*Coningsby* 1844 *Sybil* 1845 "On Peel" 1845 "On India" 1858 "The Dangers of Democracy" 1864	Leading 19th-century statesman and a novelist of merit. Founder of Conservative Party; as prime minister known for reforms and for imperialism. Speeches, which are too numerous to list, famous for brilliance, wit, sarcasm, and straightforward delivery.
	William Gladstone 1809-1898	"Warfare and Colonization" 1865 "On the Domestic and Foreign Affairs of England" 1879 "Supports the Right of Free-thinkers to Enter the House of Commons" 1883	British statesman, Liberal Party leader, advocate of many reforms, opponent of Disraeli. Gladstone considered one of leading orators of his time for his fluency, ample use of allusions, and other classic rhetorical devices.
	Thomas Henry Huxley 1825-1895	Peoples' Lectures 1855 "Examination of Darwin's *Origin of the Species*" 1862-3	Called Darwin's "Bulldog," Huxley believed in power of logical analysis and scientific experimentation as road to truth. Helped popularize theory of evolution through speeches that were at once severe, scientific, scholarly, and witty. Typically approached problems by dividing them into parts and attacking each part individually.

TABLE 7 / Great Speakers and Their Speeches *continued*

Period	Speaker	Major Speeches or Works	Characteristics and Significance
AMERICA 1600-1900	John Winthrop 1588-1649	"Little Speech on Liberty"*	Extremely influential Governor of Massachusetts Bay Colony who tried to develop theocratic government and opposed broadly based democracy. Noted for dignity and piety.
	Roger Williams 1603?-1683	*George Fox Digg'd out of his Burrowes* 1676	Clashed with Massachusetts Bay Colony on issues including separation of church and state. Established Rhode Island colony, a haven for non-Puritans. Recorded debates with Quakers in *George Fox*.
	Cotton Mather 1663-1728	"On Atheism" 1721 "Of Poetry and Style" 1726	A precocious genius, overcame a severe speech defect to become one of the leading preachers of colonial America. Author of some 500 tracts, booklets, and sermons including style guide for divinity students. Noted for pedantry, euphonious word combinations.
	Jonathan Edwards 1703-1758	Personal Narrative 1765 "Afective Versus Merely Doctrinal Religion" 1746 "The Aesthetics of Plentitude" 1765	Philosopher and minister best known for his "hellfire and brimstone" sermons and his role in colonial religious "Great Awakening."
	Benjamin Franklin 1706-1790	*Autobiography* 1771 "On the Federal Constitution" 1787	Writer, scientist, political leader, diplomat; organized debating society that became American Philosophical Society. Spoke with clarity, directness, and persuasiveness.
	Samuel Adams 1722-1803	"On American Independence" 1776	Although Adams lacked oratorical fluency and refinement, his forceful, logical, and stirring speeches helped stir up colonists before Revolution. Leading spirit of Boston Tea Party.
		*Exact date unknown	

TABLE 7 / Great Speakers and Their Speeches *continued*

Period	Speaker	Major Speeches or Works	Characteristics and Significance
	James Otis 1725-1783	"The Writs of Assistance" 1761	Fearless, logical speaker, and leader of opposition to British rule and specifically writs, which allowed unlimited right of search.
	George Washington 1732-1799	First Inaugural Address 1789 Farewell Address 1796	First U.S. President, man of action, rather than of oratory, but noted for earnestness, conviction, and ornate language.
	Patrick Henry 1736-1799	"On the Stamp Act" 1765 To the 1st Continental Congress 1774 To the Virginia Convention 1775	Patriot, lawyer, and leading orator of his day. An electrifying, emotional defender of American freedom, he coined many phrases, best known of which is "give me liberty, or give me death" that was included in speech to Virginia Convention.
	Thomas Jefferson 1743-1826	*Declaration of Independence* 1776 First Inaugural Address 1801	Third President and noted spokesman for agrarian democracy, best known for his epochal writings rather than public speaking at which he was poor. His speeches read better than they sounded to contemporaries.
	Alexander Hamilton 1755-1804	"Rutgers v. Waddington" 1779 "The Federal Constitution" 1787 "The Croswell Case" 1804	Statesman, Federalist, and first Secretary of the Treasury. Spoke in well-organized fashion with attention to transitions but had tendency to amplify and use direct questions in speeches.
	John Quincy Adams 1767-1848	Oration at Plymouth 1802 Eulogy on Lafayette 1834 The Jubilee of the Constitution 1839	Sixth President, called "Old Man Eloquent" because of gift for extemporaneous speech and debate, but was scholarly, ponderous and often sarcastic in prepared speeches.

TABLE 7 / Great Speakers and Their Speeches *continued*

Period	Speaker	Major Speeches or Works	Characteristics and Significance
	John Randolph 1773-1833	"On Internal Revenue" 1524 "On the Tariff" 1824	Statesman, orator, opponent of Henry Clay who spoke in witty, forceful, pungent fashion. Had an emphatic manner, graceful diction, and made skillful use of digression in his defense of states' rights.
	Henry Clay 1777-1852	"New Army Bill" 1813 "Emancipation of South America" 1818 "The Seminole War" 1818 "The Greek Revolution" 1824 "On the American System" "Valedictory to the Senate" 1842 Compromise Speech 1850	Statesman who is ranked as one of America's three "Golden Age" orators with Calhoun and Webster. Known as the "Great Pacificator," he supported gradual emancipation and growth of nation. Speeches noted for their charm, grace, wit, fluency, intelligence. Spoke mildly in a rich voice and established good rapport with audiences.
	John Calhoun 1782-1850	"On the Militia Bill" 1811 "On the Tariff of 1816" "On States Rights" 1833 "The Force Bill" 1833 "On the Oregon Question" 1846 "On the Slavery Question" 1850 "On the Clay Compromise Measures" 1850	Statesman, orator, bitter adversary of Webster, and supporter of states' rights, southern sectionalism, slavery. He spoke in a simple, terse, forceful, and sometimes severe way. Ideas presented in logical and profound fashion.
	Daniel Webster 1782-1852	"Plymouth Rock Address" 1820 "The Greek Revolution" 1824 "First and Second Bunker Hill Address" 1825, 1843	Statesman, lawyer and orator who favored federalism, opposed slavery and sectionalism. Called a "Herculean" orator, he was florid, bombastic, and forceful. Speaking in a deep, vibrant voice, Webster used such rhetorical

TABLE 7 / **Great Speakers and Their Speeches** *continued*

Period	Speaker	Major Speeches or Works	Characteristics and Significance
		On the Death of Jefferson and Adams 1826 "Reply to Hayne" 1830 White Murder Case 1830 Washington Centennial Speech 1832 Patchogue Speech 1840 The Clay Compromise Measure 1850 Addition to the Capitol 1851	devices as repetition, illustrations, ethical proofs, and theatricality to emphasize his voice.
	Thomas Hart Benton 1782-1858	Against the U.S. Bank 1831 The Political Career of Andrew Jackson 1837 "There is East: There is India" 1849	As senator was an effective spokesman for the West and became known for efforts to prevent Civil War. A brilliant debater who spoke in a realistic and dynamic fashion but was given to bursts of temper.
	Thaddeus Stevens 1792-1868	On the Abolition of Pennsylvania Common School System 1835 "Filth and Slime" Speech 1850	Lawyer, member of Congress, abolitionist, and leading spirit in the impeachment proceedings against Andrew Johnson. Noted for aggressive brilliance and sardonic wit.
	Ralph Waldo Emerson 1803-1882	"The American Scholar" 1837 "The Divinity School Address" 1838 "Demonology" 1839 *Essays* (collected lectures) 1841, 1844 *Representative Men* (lectures) 1850 English Traits (lectures) 1856	Called "the most steadily attractive lecturer in America" by James Russell Lowell, Emerson is as well known for his poems and essays expressing Transcendental philosophy. Lectures are noteworthy for their poetic flair, use of analogies, figures of speech, and their memorability. One of the most quoted 19th-century Americans.

TABLE 7 / Great Speakers and Their Speeches *continued*

Period	Speaker	Major Speeches or Works	Characteristics and Significance
	Abraham Lincoln 1809-1865	"A House Divided . . . ." 1858 Debates with Stephan Douglas 1858 Address, Cooper Union 1860 Farewell Address at Springfield, Illinois 1861 First Inaugural Address 1861 Gettysburg Address 1863 Second Inaugural Address 1865	Civil War President, known as "The Great Emancipator." Spoke with directness, sincerity, and simplicity. Discarded rhetoric and oratorical frills for honest fervor and gentle wit.
	Stephen A. Douglas 1813-1860	"The Kansas-Nebraska Bill" 1854 Debates with Lincoln 1858	Senator called "The Little Giant," originator of idea of "popular sovereignity" for citizens of new territories. Worked hard to avoid outbreak of Civil War. Spoke with fluent, energetic, forceful voice.
	Henry Ward Beecher 1813-1887	"Lectures to Young Men" 1841 "Lecture to the American & Foreign Anti-Slavery Society" 1851 "Liverpool Address" 1863 "The Fort Sumter Flag-Raising Address" 1865 "Memorial Sermon for Lincoln" 1865 "Yale Lectures on Preaching" 1872	One of the best known and most highly regarded pulpit orators of his time. Strong patriotism, religious sentiments, and anti-slavery views conveyed in extremely effective style that resembled conversation with audience.
	Robert Green Ingersoll 1833-1899	"Plumed Knight"—nomination speech for James Blaine 1876	Lawyer and orator. H.W. Beecher called him "most brilliant speaker of the English tongue of all the men on the

TABLE 7 / Great Speakers and Their Speeches *continued*

Period	Speaker	Major Speeches or Works	Characteristics and Significance
		"The Gods" 1872 "Some Mistakes on Moses" 1879 "Why I am an Agnostic" 1896 "Superstition" 1898	globe" despite his anti-religious beliefs and lectures questioning fundamental Christian ideas. Eloquent, witty, and provocative, Ingersoll's lectures were staple of American literature for several generations.
	Russell Conwell	"Acres of Diamonds" 1861	Baptist minister whose repetition of this one speech on art of moneymaking raised enough cash for founding of Temple University.
THE TWENTIETH CENTURY	Woodrow Wilson 1856-1924 (U.S.A.)	Speech at Jackson Day Dinner 1912 Message to Senate on Neutrality 1914 Address to Congress, Asking for Declaration of War 1917 Address to Congress, Fourteen Points 1918 For the League of Nations 1919	Lawyer, professor of economy and history, president of Princeton, and twenty-eighth President of the United States. His speeches are considered among the finest ever given by an American. They are orderly, logical, intellectual expressions of his ideals.
	Clarence S. Darrow 1857-1938 (U.S.A.)	Leopold and Loeb Case 1924 Scopes ("Monkey") Trial 1925 "I Do Not Believe in the Law of Hate" 1926	Famous criminal lawyer whose deceptive countrified manner, use of emotional appeals, repetition, and simple language helped him achieve success.
	Theodore Roosevelt 1858-1919 (U.S.A.)	"The Strenuous Life" 1899 "National & Industrial Peace" 1902 "The Man with the Muck Rake" 1906 Khartoum & Guildhall Speeches 1910	Twenty-sixth President and leader in fight for civil reforms. Speech style, which was brusque, conversational, vehement, and sincere, set the style for generations to come.

TABLE 7 / Great Speakers and Their Speeches *continued*

Period	Speaker	Major Speeches or Works	Characteristics and Significance
		"The Right of the People to Rule" 1912 Columbia Speech 1912 Plattsburg Speech 1915 "The Flag on the Firing Line" 1917	
	William Jennings Bryan 1860-1925 (U.S.A.)	"The Cross of Gold" 1896 "America's Mission" 1899 "Imperialism" 1900 "Madison Square Speech" 1900 "The Prince of Peace" (lecture tour) Scopes Trial, 1925	Known as "The Silver-Tongued Orator" and "The Great Commoner" this Populist is known for his belief in free and unlimited coinage of silver, about which he made some 600 speeches. Several campaigns for presidency failed, but his gift as a speaker with a magnificent voice, and use of full range of rhetorical devices (analogy, antithesis, figures of speech, etc.) helped keep his popularity alive. Last important speeches delivered for prosecution in Scopes trial, where his anti-evolutionary views were ridiculed sharply by Darrow (see above).
	Mohandas Karmchand Gandhi 1869-1948 (India)	Nonviolence is the First Article of My Faith 1922 Speech in London 1931	Leader of India's movement to gain independence of England. Gandhi's nonviolent philosophy was reflected in the gentle, earnest, hypnotic delivery of speeches.
	Winston Churchill 1874-1965 (England)	On the Munich Agreement 1938 First Statement as Prime Minister ("Blood, Sweat and Tears") 1940 Speech on Dunkirk 1940 Tribute to Royal Air Force 1940 "V for Victory" speech 1941	One of the great English statesmen of the century, a brilliant, inspirational leader, and masterly writer and speaker. His phrases such as "This was their finest hour" (1940), and "the Iron Curtain" (1946) are only a few of many that are commonly used to this day. His wit, use of analogy, metaphor, and anecdote make his speeches as exciting to read as they were to hear.

TABLE 7 / Great Speakers and Their Speeches *continued*

Period	Speaker	Major Speeches or Works	Characteristics and Significance
		Speech to Lord Mayor's Day Luncheon 1942 Tribute to Roosevelt 1945 Address at Westminister College (Missouri)—"The Sinews of Peace" 1946	
	Douglas MacArthur 1880-1964 (U.S.A.)	Address on leaving Corregidor, the Philippines 1942 Address to Congress 1951 Speech to Republican National Convention 1952	Renowned World War II general whose 1942 vow, "I shall return," captured spirit of times. His address to Congress on his dismissal from Korean Command known for phrase, "Old soldiers never die . . ." A forceful, emotional, vivid speaker.
	Franklin Delano Roosevelt 1882-1945 (U.S.A.)	"Happy Warrior" Speech 1924 First Inaugural Speech 1933 Fireside Chats 1933-45 (on radio) "Hand that Held the Dagger" 1941 War Message to Congress 1941 Fourth Inaugural Address 1945	Thirty-second President of the United States and nation's leader during Depression and World War II. Famous for brilliant speeches in conversational but forceful style that was rich in memorable phrases, vivid figures of speech, and wit. First President to make use of radio on a large scale.
	Harry S. Truman 1884-1973 (U.S.A.)	First Message to Congress 1945 Declaration on Atomic Energy (with Clement Atlee and Mackenzie King) 1945	Thirty-third President of the United States during dawn of Atomic Age and beginning of the Cold War between East and West. Noted for his plain-spoken, commonsensical, and blunt speech laced with earthy wit.

TABLE 7 / Great Speakers and Their Speeches *continued*

Period	Speaker	Major Speeches or Works	Characteristics and Significance
		Greek-Turkish Aid Message to Congress 1947 Inaugural Address (Point Four Program) 1949	
	Adolf Hitler 1889-1945 (Germany)	*Mein kampf* (Complete edition) 1940 Address at Sports Palast 1938 Proclamation to his Troops 1941 Speech to Reichstag 1942	German dictator (1933-44), founder and leader of National Socialist (Nazi) party. Speeches, which often verged on hysterical, were melodramatic and theatrical. In shrill voice and clipped phrases, denounced World War I treaties, expounded German "greatness," and incited hatred of Jews, and other "enemies."
	Charles de Gaulle 1890-1970 (France)	Broadcast to French people 1940 The Future of France 1963 On the European Common Market 1967	General of Free French during World War II, later President of France. Aimed to keep spirit of French alive during German occupation ("the flame of French resistance shall not die . . . 1940) and to rebuild national greatness as President. Considered the finest French orator of the century.
	Nikita Sergeyevich Khrushchev 1894-1971 (U.S.S.R.)	"The Personality Cult and Its Consequences," also called "The Secret Report"—delivered at Twentieth All-Union Party Congress 1956	Russian Communist leader and first secretary of the party (1953-1964). His 'Secret Report' denounced the personality cult that had grown up around rule and policies of Stalin. Speech had widespread effect within U.S.S.R. and nations of East Europe.
	Everett McKinley Dirksen 1896-1969 (U.S.A.)	"The State of the Union: A Republican Appraisal" 1966 "A Republic if You Can Keep It" 1968	Republican senator from Illinois and the eloquent voice of his party. Known for his colorful, anecdotal speeches.

TABLE 7 / Great Speakers and Their Speeches *continued*

Period	Speaker	Major Speeches or Works	Characteristics and Significance
	Adlai Ewing Stevenson 1900-1965 (U.S.A.)	Nomination Acceptance Speech 1952 *A Call to Greatness* 1954 *Putting First Things First* 1960	Lawyer, governor of Illinois, twice candidate for the presidency (1952 and 1956) and ambassador to the United Nations. Considered the most literate and wittiest Presidential candidate of the century but humor, use of classical and other allusions, won him name of "egg-head" and may have contributed to election defeats.
	Lyndon Baines Johnson 1908-1973 (U.S.A.)	State of the Union Address 1966 "Vietnam: The Cause of Human Freedom" 1966 "A Stronger NATO" 1966 "The Need for Scholars" 1966	Senate leader and then thirty-sixth President of the United States. Favored "The Great Society" domestically and was responsible for largest U.S. involve-ment in Vietnam. Speeches characterized by simple, frontier-style directness and dry wit; often by elevated religious fervor.
	Richard Milhous Nixon 1913- (U.S.A.)	"Checkers" Speech 1952 "Kitchen Debate" with Khruschev 1959 Nixon-Kennedy Debates 1960 "The Pursuit of Peace" 1969 Second Inaugural Address 1973	Congressman, Vice-President under Eisenhower (1952-1960), President (1969-), Nixon defended his repu-tation in the "Checkers" speech to retain place on Republican ticket. Effective-ness as speaker and debater due in part to participation in high school and col-lege debating societies. Speeches are usually simple, well-organized, direct, and concrete.
	John Fitzgerald Kennedy 1917-1963 (U.S.A.)	Nixon-Kennedy Debates 1960 Inaugural Address 1961 Address to the People of West Berlin 1963 Address to the United Nations 1963	Thirty-sixth President of the United States, known for belief in strong mili-tary posture and support of civil rights movement. Speeches notable for charm, grace, gift for effective phrasing, wit, and personal style of delivery.

TABLE 7 / Great Speakers and Their Speeches *continued*

Period	Speaker	Major Speeches or Works	Characteristics and Significance
	Spiro T. Agnew 1918- (U.S.A.)	On television news coverage 1969 On newspapers and other media 1973	Vice-President and most noted speech-maker of Nixon administration. Force-ful, blunt, witty, fond of alliterative phrases that sting the opposition.
	Fidel Castro 1927- (Cuba)	"Give Me Liberty or Give Me Death" 1960 May Day Address 1970	Leader of Cuban Communist govern-ment. Hypnotic orator who can speak for hours at a time in tones alternately boastful, emotional, rhythmic, and above all, magnetic.
	Martin Luther King, Jr. 1929-1968 (U.S.A.)	"I Have a Dream . . ." 1965	Most renowned U.S. civil rights leader, King was a gifted orator who spoke with exceptional clarity and religious fervor. He employed such rhetorical devices as contrast, repetition, analogy, proofs, and built to a series of effective and inspirational climaxes.

General Index

Index of Works in the Annotated
Listing of Basic References

D